THE EU'S SEARCH FOR A STRATEGIC ROLE

ESDP AND ITS IMPLICATIONS

FOR TRANSATLANTIC

RELATIONS

Edited by Esther Brimmer

Brimmer, Esther, ed. *The EU's Search for a Strategic Role: ESDP and Its Implications for Transatlantic Relations.* Washington, D.C.: Center for Transatlantic Relations, 2002

Center for Transatlantic Relations
EU Center Washington, D.C.
The Paul H. Nitze School of Advanced International Studies
The Johns Hopkins University
1717 Massachusetts, N.W., Suite 525
Washington, D.C. 20036
Tel. (202) 663-5880
Fax (202) 663-5879
Email: transatlantic.sais-jhu.edu
http://transatlantic.sais-jhu.edu

Cover photograph: The photograph from the United Nations archive shows Yugoslav troops on patrol with the United Nations Emergency Force (UNEF) in El Arish, Egypt, in January 1957 (53061 UN/DPI). UNEF was the first UN peacekeeping force. Peacekeeping is not mentioned in the UN Charter; it was an innovative response to a security need. Forty years later, the disintegration of Yugoslavia would be the impetus for creating ESDP to improve the European Union's capacity for peace operations.

Table of Contents

tial of the transatlantic partnership as a factor for stability in the century to come. Some adjustment is required on both sides, in terms of capabilities, but also of perceptions.

As far as perceptions of threats are concerned, for most Americans, 11 September has changed everything. Until then, America could always rely on geography to protect the homeland. The brutal attacks on its own soil have overturned that perception. Europe had been used for centuries to the idea of threats on its soil, until very recently. The fall of the Berlin Wall left the Europeans with a new sense of security, which the terrorist threat has dented but not abolished. Closing the perception gap requires a better mutual understanding of the nature of the threats posed to our open societies by ruthless opponents, ready to use terrorism and possibly weapons of mass destruction.

The question then arises how to deal with them. The U.S. response was swift and forceful. Europeans supported the use of force and still do. But they make two points, which bear repeating. The first is that a military response alone will not solve the problem of terrorism. The second is that even the strongest country in the world needs partners and allies, not simple followers. A true partnership requires dialogue and mutual respect. But it also requires both sides to be convinced of its benefits.

This raises the question of the balance of contributions. In terms of political and security capabilities, the burden of adjustment clearly lies on European shoulders. Through the ESDP, the Europeans are determined to develop the tools the EU needs to become a stronger and more equal partner for the U.S. and to be able to act decisively when and where needed, in close co-operation with NATO. That does not mean trying to equal the U.S. military build-up. But it must mean Europeans spending more or spending better—and spending better means integrating more. Painful choices will have to be made if Europe is to live up to her security ambitions. But more painful still would be to do nothing. To do nothing, to avoid the hard choices ahead, would guarantee a steady decline in European capabilities to the point where it would be ever more difficult to operate alongside the U.S. and to remain relevant as a strategic actor. If and when the tough decisions required to that effect are taken, this will be good news for Europe and for the U.S.

There is a perception that Europe offers too much talk and too little action, while the reverse applies to the U.S. What is the European side of the equation? After 11 September, Europe delivered action as well as words. In Afghanistan, six thousand European troops stand shoulder to shoulder with their American partners. Europe, together with the US, plays a leading role in reconstruction and nation building. The fight against terrorism has led to a flurry of activity in judicial and police co-operation. In the Balkans the EU is progressively taking on a more active role, with the full backing and support of the U.S. Of the 58,000 peacekeeping troops currently in the Balkans, 38,000 are Europeans. As in Afghanistan, the financial burden is being shared, with the EU by far the largest financial donor.

In the Middle East the U.S. and Europe have worked closely together. The co-operation within the Quartet should be the model that inspires us. Policymakers on both sides of the Atlantic share to a very wide extent the same vision of a just and durable settlement. We must concentrate now on mechanisms allowing that shared vision to be realized.

We need to take courage from our successes and apply them elsewhere. A sustained collaborative approach is needed on other common priorities: Africa; poverty; epidemic and pandemic disease, and the environment. These are issues that threaten our interests, our values, and our security. But they are also issues on which Europe and the United States have the capacity to lead an "axis of good." This takes us far from a somewhat sterile debate about the choice between "hard" and "soft" security. Our real objective should be "smart" security.

Even the best of friends do not agree on all matters. The sign of a mature and equal relationship is not the absence of conflict but the capacity to deal with it in a responsible manner. The European desire for the U.S. to be more committed to multilateral solutions is not a case of Lilliputians trying to tie down the superpower Gulliver. It is based instead on three factors.

Firstly, because of the EU practice of shared sovereignty, the belief in collective action comes naturally to Europeans. More than forty years of experience has taught Europeans that multilateral solutions are an alternative to war and that sovereignty shared is sovereignty revitalized. Secondly, Europeans are convinced that global problems—whether they are economic, environmental or political—require genuinely global solutions. Goods, services, people circulate more than ever. Greenhouse gas emissions do not respect borders. Nor do terrorists or criminals. Conflicts spread from one country to another; financial crises have spillover effects worldwide. And thirdly, a commitment to genuine multilateralism is a long-term investment in security. If the weakest and poorest feel that their voice will not be heard then they will soon be the angriest.

Forty years ago the then President of the United States proposed a "declaration of interdependence" between a united Europe and the United States. Speaking at the Independence Hall in Philadelphia, President Kennedy spoke of "a concrete Atlantic partnership, a mutually beneficial partnership between the new union now emerging in Europe and the old American Union." Transatlantic interdependence did indeed grow, in the economic, security and political spheres. The intervening forty years have seen the disappearance of a Cold War threat that was stable and unifying in its impact on the transatlantic link. Now we face new and unpredictable threats.

Today it is not only Europe and the United States that are interdependent. We live in an increasingly interdependent world. Economics, security and politics are bound together in a complex web. No one is completely sheltered from these interdependencies, not even the most powerful. We must begin to see our reliance on one another as a blessing not a curse. Common cause spurs us to collective action. Of course, collective action comes at a price: hard work, patience, a willingness to listen, and sometimes compromise. But given the nature of the challenges of the century to come I am convinced that collective action is our best hope of mastering our destiny and achieving progress.

Today, human events dictate that it is necessary not to dissolve but to strengthen the political, security and economic bands that connect us. To that end we want more Europe, not less America.

This book about the transatlantic implications of the emerging European Security and Defense Policy is both timely and valuable as a contribution to the ongoing debate on the future of the transatlantic partnership in the 21st century. A joint venture between the Center for Transatlantic Relations at John Hopkins University and the Bundeswehr Center for Analyses and Studies, associating scholars and experts from both sides of the Atlantic, it exemplifies the sort of constructive and frank dialogue that is needed at this important juncture for the transatlantic partnership. More than ever it is essential that Americans and Europeans make it a priority to talk to each other rather than about each other.

Introduction

The European Security and Defense Policy is hardly the first effort by the members of the European Union to develop a military capacity. Decades before there was a Union, when the European Coal and Steel Community were still new, there was an effort to build European Defense Cooperation. Although that effort failed in 1954, there was a continuing, if episodic, interest in bringing together the foreign and security policies of countries that had decided to pool sovereignty in the European project.

The grand project of European integration has always had at its core the goal of improving security on the European continent, beginning in the 1950s with reconcilation between Germany and France, Italy and the Benelux countries. Successive expansion during ensuing decades of what is now the European Union to include the United Kingdom, Ireland, Greece, Spain, Portugal, Sweden, Denmark, Finland and Austria widened the zone of stability supporting functional integration across most of western Europe. The fall 2002 decision of the EU to admit ten more countries is the latest step in this process. The EU has grown both by widening its scope and deepening the level of integration among its members. Through enlargement and the conclusion of a series of treaties, the EU has taken on increasingly complex initiatives from creating the Single Market to launching the euro. With the Treaty of Amsterdam, the EU has added a High Representative for Foreign and Security Policy to its existing Commissioner for External Affairs. The dynamism of these offices, the significance of European economic power, and size of European development aid give the EU many of the classic tools of diplomatic power.

Yet diplomatic power has usually been backed by access to military power. Member states have been grappling with the question: should the EU develop military power, and if so, how and for what purpose? The European Security and Defense Policy (ESDP) is the most recent effort to add a military aspect to the EU's international profile, although it encompasses a broader range of tools, including policing and crisis management capabilities. Some of the EU member states already have an important international presence as national governments, and most participate in collective defense as members of the North Atlantic Treaty Organization (NATO). The close relationships among the United States and EU member states mean that any substantial change in the EU's international role would affect the U.S. This volume explores the impact of ESDP on transatlantic relations and asks whether ESDP is a mechanism to project European power or a process to enhance European integration and help spread the EU model of stability to regions in or near Europe. EU member states answer this question differently. Member states have put forward various interpretations of ESDP since the 1998 St. Malo agreement between the United Kingdom and France which gave new impetus to ESDP, but whatever form it takes, ESDP affects Europeans' and Americans' perceptions of each other, and will be part of the background for relations in the future. Whether or not ESDP is successful, it will shape attitudes towards European security policy for the next several years.

The book considers both progress on ESDP and prospects for its future. Authors:

- Explore the strategic trends behind ESDP and the relationship between the EU and NATO;

- Identify possible implications of ESDP for global security architecture, especially in the area of peace operations;

- Discuss European and American viewpoints with regard to the future of the transatlantic partnership; and

- Offer recommendations for addressing some of the challenges facing ESDP and the EU in its search for an expanded security role.

These four elements underpin the volume. The first section analyzes ESDP and its role in the European Union and provides context for the rest of the book. Gerd Föhrenbach's opening chapter introduces the EU's preference for security through engagement. Sir Michael Quinlan looks at a particular kind of engagement, enlargement, and evaluates its impact on ESDP. As the EU expands its security role, it must find its place among international organizations. Marc Otte addresses ESDP's relations with other institutions. These different institutions make various demands on EU members. Antonio Missiroli considers which capacities are being developed under the rubric of ESDP. Ralph Thiele concludes the section with an overview of how ESDP might fit into Europe's efforts to project power.

The next section considers ESDP and international security, including relations with Russia and contributions to peacekeeping and peace operations. Tuomas Forsberg describes Russia's role in ESDP. Esther Brimmer considers ways in which ESDP could contribute to international peacekeeping.

The final section addresses transatlantic relations. Bruno Tertrais takes on the "division of labor" debate, while Peter van Ham explores the impact of the United States on the development of ESDP. Daniel Hamilton concludes the section with an American perspective on European efforts to project power.

Although the book is intended to form a whole, each chapter is solely the view of the author. Differences of interpretation remain and are not homogenized into a consensus. The authors met as a group three times in 2002 to share ideas, but not to form a single opinion. The conclusion highlights key findings. Authors' recommendations are developed more fully in the chapters.

ESDP and European Union

Security Through Engagement: The Worldview Underlying ESDP

Gerd Föhrenbach*

Introduction

At the Cologne European Council in June 1999, the fifteen member states of the European Union (EU) embarked on a historic journey which is to provide them over the next few years with a common policy on security and defense matters. The aim is to strengthen the EU's role in international politics by rendering the Union capable of independent action in the whole spectrum of non-military and military crisis management.

The position of the United States on the European Security and Defense Policy (ESDP), as the project has become known, has always been ambivalent. While both the Clinton and the Bush administrations welcomed the efforts of the Europeans to improve the capabilities of their armed forces, doubts persist in Washington with regard to ESDP's potentially divisive effect on the North Atlantic Treaty Organization (NATO) and the willingness of the Europeans to make major investments in their militaries.

At the Helsinki European Council in December 1999, EU members agreed to the European Headline Goal of being capable, as soon as 2003, of deploying 50-60,000 troops within 60 days and sustaining those forces for at least one year. The forces' mission will be to implement the so-called Petersberg tasks.[1] This ambitious military goal and the debates about its achievement have attracted the attention of many observers on both sides of the Atlantic, but it has also caused a certain imbalance in the way ESDP has been perceived. There is a tendency to focus on the military aspects of ESDP and to neglect, at the same time, the project's overall concept, which has many more facets.

This essay will analyze the worldview and the notions on which ESDP and the Common Foreign and Security Policy (CFSP), of

---

*The views expressed in this article are solely those of the author.

which ESDP is but one element, are based. It will, firstly, put the two projects in a historical perspective, which is necessary to understand both the achievements of the EU and the challenges facing it. Subsequently, the analysis will concentrate on the three core functions that ESDP and CFSP have to fulfill within the EU and, then, on some noteworthy legal aspects. Finally, topics such as the threat assessment underlying ESDP, the capabilities issue, the importance of the transatlantic link, and the impact of September 11 will be discussed.

The Historical Perspective

The creation of the European Economic Community (EEC) and its successor, the European Union, has to be seen as an attempt by Germany, France and other countries to learn from history. Instead of continuing the politics of coalition-building and balance-of-power after the horrors of World War II, the Europeans recognized the need to cooperate. Over the years and decades, the cooperative structures which the former enemies developed in the framework of the EEC and the EU provided essential prerequisites for unheard-of prosperity and lasting stability in Western Europe. As German foreign minister Joschka Fischer put it in a speech on the future of the EU, "The core of the concept of Europe after 1945 was and still is a rejection of the European balance-of-power principle and the hegemonic ambitions of individual states that had emerged following the Peace of Westphalia in 1648."[2]

After the failure in 1954 of an initiative to establish an integrated European force, the so-called European Defense Community, European leaders decided to focus instead on cooperation in the economic field.[3] Today, the EU is still primarily an economic community, albeit a very successful one.

Thus, the term "European Union" suggests a picture of a unified Europe which, in reality, hardly exists. In important political fields, the EU is still made up of fifteen individual nation states. Many "classical" policy areas such as foreign and security policy and domestic affairs have remained under the tutelage of the national governments. After all, the EU was not intended to be a crisis management organization (which explains some of its perceived deficiencies in that area, see below).

Europe's cooperation and integration is a dynamic work in progress. Currently, the Union is preparing for, or has already launched, four projects of historic dimensions: economic and monetary union, enlargement to the east, reform of the EU's institutions, and ESDP. Each of these undertakings alone would be a major challenge for the Union. Together, they promise to fundamentally change the face of Europe beyond recognition over the next several years. That is, if the projects can be realized as planned, which should not be taken for granted. The future success of the EU is by no means pre-ordained.

The Functions of ESDP and CFSP

Against this background it becomes apparent that the Union's CFSP in general and ESDP in particular have three functions.

The institutional development function

The EU has a unique organizational structure that is unlike any other international organization. NATO, for example, is a military alliance centering on an integrated military command that is answerable to an intergovernmental body, the North Atlantic Council. By contrast, the Union the Europeans have been building is a regulatory institution which formulates, implements and enforces rules, norms, and regulations by way of a long-winded process of deliberation and consultation.[4]

European integration is an on-going process. In some policy areas, integration has progressed quite far, notably in those fields such as agricultural policy and the common market which belong to the so-called first, integrated pillar of the European Union. Under this pillar, member states have largely given up sovereignty and transferred it to the supranational institutions of the EU. Under the second and third pillars, i.e. the areas of foreign and security policy and justice and home affairs, there have been some efforts aimed at increasing intergovernmental cooperation for many years, yet for a number of reasons they have yielded only limited results.

With the advent of new security challenges, both external and internal, after the end of the Cold War and against the background of the political, economic, and social phenomenon which has been labeled "globalization," it has become clear that European cooperation in foreign and security policy has to be developed further.

It is in this respect that the institutional development function of the CFSP and ESDP plays an important role. Foreign and security policy are fields which have traditionally been under the control of the national governments. However, the notion that individual European governments can act in these areas in an independent, "sovereign" way has become increasingly hollow. Solutions for most of today's and tomorrow's security challenges can no longer be found at national level, but only at international level. As a report by the United States Department of Defense put it, the "development of a foreign and security policy for the EU is a natural, even an inevitable, part of the development of broader European integration."[5] In this sense, ESDP has to be seen as one building-block in a piecemeal process in the course of which sovereignty is transferred step by step from the member states to the Union.

Nevertheless, one also has to recognize the limits of the ESDP project. Javier Solana, the High Representative for the CFSP, has pointed out that the purpose of CFSP and ESDP is not to replace fifteen national foreign ministries and fifteen foreign policies with a single EU policy run from Brussels. Rather, his task is "to identify what is common to these national policies."[6] Moreover, EU member states have different strategic traditions. Countries like the United Kingdom and France are rather active militarily while others like Germany and the formerly neutral states are much more reticent about the use of force. The differences and gaps in the strategic cultures of the member states are, and will continue to be, an essential factor determining the scope of the EU's international role. Thus, CFSP and ESDP can also be understood as an internal learning and development process by the member states whose objective is to find ways to pursue shared aims in an increasingly interdependent world, thereby gradually adjusting the EU's internal structures to 21st century security challenges.

The defense function

During the wars in former Yugoslavia what had been known all along became painfully obvious: that the European Union was an economic giant, but a political dwarf. Europe was incapable of preventing a humanitarian catastrophe in its own region. The carnage in the Balkans made it clear that the Union had to develop its own mechanisms for crisis management. Also, there was a fear of being abandoned by the Americans, which was already a driving force behind the development of the Petersberg task in 1992 and has led some EU members to regard ESDP as a hedge against the risk of U.S. disengagement from the European continent.

EU leaders agreed at the European Councils at Cologne and Helsinki to develop a comprehensive concept for crisis management that includes both civilian and military means and puts particular emphasis on crisis prevention. The military side of the undertaking, the European Headline Goal, is well-known and much debated. Less well-known are the many promising facets on the civilian side.

As the world's largest provider of development assistance and the biggest trading partner, the EU has significant influence in many regions all over the globe. Therefore, the Union is particularly well-suited for dealing with conflict prevention. The Union's capabilities in this respect include, beside development assistance, a variety of tools such as diplomatic instruments, trade policy mechanisms, cooperation agreements, and humanitarian assistance.[7] With these tools at its disposal, the Union is able to influence, and by implication to defend against, a potential risk long before it grows into a crisis.

One prominent example of how successful the EU's conflict prevention capabilities can be is the stabilization of Eastern Europe after 1989. In a speech in Berlin, the then U.S. secretary of state James A. Baker III pointed out the importance of the European Community to serve "as an open door to the East."[8] Apart from the wars in the Balkans, the EU's policies and its attractiveness as a political and economic partner have helped in the rest of Eastern Europe to defuse many ethnic, political, or social problems that could have triggered crises.

Civilian capacities also feature prominently in the EU's mechanisms for acute crisis management. By 2003 the EU intends to be able to provide, inter alia, up to 5,000 police officers (1,000 within 30 days), up to 2,000 civil protection specialists and up to 200 civil administration experts for international missions. Their task will be to strengthen the rule of law, administrative structures and civil protection in countries outside the Union.

To put it in a nutshell, the EU will soon offer "one-stop shopping" for political, diplomatic, economic, social as well as military instruments to exert influence or put pressure on the parties to a conflict. The EU's concept of "one-stop shopping" for crisis prevention and management is a novelty among international organizations. It shows that the notion of "defense" underlying ESDP reaches far beyond the establishment of a rapid reaction force. ESDP is an all-encompassing approach whose special emphasis on crisis prevention and the civilian aspects of crisis management is a marked difference to NATO. The EHG is but one level in this concept.

The Union's massive engagement in Macedonia nicely illustrates the potential benefits of "one-stop shopping." The EU has been able to support that Balkan country in many areas ranging from inter-ethnic dialogue to local government development to trade preferences. Because the EU's civilian conflict prevention capabilities have been applied in a timely and focused manner—and in close cooperation with NATO, which oversees the military part of the mission—the risk of civil war has been substantially reduced.

The strategic function

There is a growing awareness that the EU's increasing involvement in world affairs provides it with a sense of mission. To be sure, the EU is not alone in promoting democracy, the rule of law, and an open trading system. But, as Solana says, "we are unique in combining our commitment to these goals with the unparalleled degree of aid and assistance that we collectively give and with our attachment to a genuine and comprehensive multilateralism in international relations."[9] The "European vision," as he calls it, is one that "combines globalization with multilateralism." Those who believe that multilateralism restricts national freedom of action are told that "[w]e must not think that there is an inevitable trade-off between effectiveness and inclusiveness" because acting alone diminishes legitimacy and effectiveness in the long run.[10] Being a law-based institution itself, the EU strives to use its power for establishing (legal) standards in international relations. International law and multilateral treaties and agreements are considered crucial means for enhancing order in world affairs. In short, ESDP underscores the EU's strategy to seek "security through engagement."[11]

This vision is echoed by Romano Prodi, the president of the European Commission, who is endeavoring to "make our voice heard, to make our actions count"[12] on the world stage. British prime minister Tony Blair has even declared that the strategic objective of the EU is to become a "superpower"[13] (while simultaneously rejecting the notion of a "superstate").

Naturally, the strategic aspirations of ESDP have caused unease in Washington, which does not want to lose influence in Europe. However, as will be discussed later in this chapter, it is in America's interest to have a more capable European partner, even at the strategic level. American grand strategy for the past 100 years has been based on the notions of denying the rise of any Eurasian or Asian hegemon and, even more importantly in the context of this analysis, the establishment of a transatlantic-Eurasian security system, including Russia and China, that promotes peace, stability, and prosperity. The latter objective certainly cannot be achieved without the support of the nations in the region, and the EU could become the natural partner of the U.S.[14]

Some Legal Aspects of ESDP and CFSP

The Treaty of Amsterdam, which came into force on 1 May 1999, contains a number of provisions on CFSP and ESDP. As article 11 paragraph 1 of the Treaty on European Union (TEU) states,

> "The Union shall define and implement a common foreign and security policy covering *all areas of foreign and security policy*, the objectives of which shall be:
> —to safeguard the common values, *fundamental interests*, independence and integrity of the Union *in conformity with the principles of the United Nations Charter* (. . .)."[15]

The fact that the treaty explicitly refers to "all areas of foreign and security policy" implies that in principle the TEU does not contain any limitations—be they regional or functional—for the CFSP. However, ESDP currently only refers to the Petersberg tasks included in the TEU in the 2001 Treaty of Nice (which has yet to come into force).[16] A transferral of the Article 5 military assistance commitment of the treaty of the Western European Union presently does not seem to be politically feasible. The Union's "fundamental interests" are not listed specifically, but it can be assumed that they go beyond the national interests of the individual member states. The phrase "in conformity with the principles of the United Nations Charter" suggests that the CFSP should be seen as being subordinate to the principles of the United Nations.

Moreover, EU members have committed themselves to solidarity. Article 11 paragraph 2 TEU stipulates that the members "shall support the Union's external and security policy actively and unreservedly in a spirit of loyalty and mutual solidarity." EU member states "shall refrain from any action which is contrary to the interests of the Union or likely to impair its effectiveness as a cohesive force in international relations." Specifically, article 19 paragraph 2 requires those EU members which are also elected members of the U.N. Security Council (2001-02 Ireland, 2003-04 Germany and Spain) to concert and keep the other EU members fully informed. EU members which are permanent members of the Security Council, i.e. France and the United Kingdom, must ensure the defense of the positions and the interests of the EU.

A decision on the use of an EU military force has to be made unanimously (article 23 TEU). Abstentions do not prevent the adoption of such a decision. The requirement to be able to act only after unanimous decisions has two implications. If an EU force is deployed, it will always be supported politically by all member states. Since all EU member states are democracies that share common values, broad democratic support is guaranteed, which in turn provides the mission with legitimacy. However, much more problematic than a unanimous decision to intervene with an EU force (even with abstentions) would be a situation when some EU members undertake an intervention without the approval of the other members. Were such a situation to occur, it would damage ESDP and the Union as a whole. As the exclusive, sovereign right to decide whether or not to use its armed forces still rests with each individual member state, a consensus among EU members will remain essential for future EU-led missions, but there may occur tensions between militarily activist countries and more restrained members.

Finally, while referring to the principles of the U.N. charter, the TEU does not explicitly require the Union to obtain a U.N. Security Council mandate for interventions. However, a Security Council authorization will always be politically desirable, but it does not seem to be a conditio sine qua non for all cases. The old legalistic principle of non-intervention has undergone significant changes. Indeed, during the 1990s EU members contributed actively to rework the principle insofar as interventions may sometimes be necessary in order to prevent a humanitarian catastrophe or protect collective interests. The Kosovo air campaign of 1999 showed that European states were willing to act even without a Security Council mandate because the humanitarian crisis in that region and the threat to stability created a sense of overwhelming urgency in the Union.[17]

Security Challenges and Military Capabilities

Europe's security situation has changed profoundly since 1989. Gone is the threat of a massive Soviet attack through the Fulda Gap. However, despite many summit communiqués which contain references to the new security problems, Europeans still have not fully realized, let alone drawn all the necessary consequences from, the complexity of the changes. It is true that information on the security challenges is readily available. Solana, to give but one example, points inter alia to tensions in Eastern Europe; instability in the Balkans, the Mediterranean, and the Middle East; the threat of criminals or terrorists armed with weapons of mass destruction (WMD); large-scale computer sabotage; environmental risks; and the scourge of organized crime.[18] Yet, as the German Bundesnachrichtendienst (Federal Intelligence Service) has stated with regard to the proliferation of WMD, "the general public is largely unaware of the intensity with which some countries pursue their WMD projects."[19] Notwithstanding some public statements shortly after the shock of September 11, political and opinion leaders in Europe have as yet largely avoided engaging in a public discussion on how to respond to the strategic security challenges (although the terrorist attacks would have provided an opportunity to do so). Despite the fact that Europe is located much closer to most of the potential trouble spots, the new strategic threats have attracted minimal attention at best.

This is in stark contrast to how Americans have perceived security developments, even before September 2001. A key reason why European and U.S. security perceptions have been diverging is probably the fact that the sense of security which Europe's political élites felt under the U.S. nuclear umbrella during the Cold War still persists. The belief that America will always, quasi-automatically, protect Europe's security is, to put it succinctly, so deeply-rooted that Europeans have neglected their own defense efforts (while, at the same time, often denouncing those of the Americans as being "out of proportion").[20]

ESDP is a step in the right direction. During the 1990s, European defense budgets constantly decreased to an average of less than two percent of the gross domestic product. Yet, over a longer time even constant defense spending in fact means a decline. Besides, an increase in the number of operations conducted requires larger budget shares to be allocated to operational costs to the detriment of the budgets for investment, research and development. Since an increase in European defense expenditures does not seem likely, better spending is necessary. In this respect, the role of ESDP as a capability-driven process is to encourage and facilitate the processes of developing multinational capabilities, of increasing task-sharing among the national forces, and of pooling resources and assets.[21]

The Transatlantic Link

It would be pointless to deny that on a number of political, economic, and environmental issues the EU and the U.S. have different opinions. At the same time, it is also inappropriate to argue, like Robert Kagan, an influential, conservative thinker in the U.S., that "[i]t is time to stop pretending that Europeans and Americans share a common view of the world, or even that they occupy the same world."[22] Since Europe and the U.S. are both being confronted with the security challenges of the 21st century, they need each other more than ever. America and Europe share the values on which the structures are founded that have sustained peace, freedom, and prosperity in the North Atlantic region for so long.

For Europe, a close relationship to the U.S. is essential for two reasons above all. Firstly, American involvement as "a European power,"[23] as Richard Holbrooke once wrote, has been the key factor that helped to break the cycle of war in the Western part of the continent after 1945. The presence of the Americans puts the Europeans under pressure to end their historical rivalries. (Ironically, the U.S. security guarantee for Europe also contributed to today's weakness insofar as the Europeans were not required to provide for their security on their own). Secondly, the close relationship that has developed between the U.S. and Germany diminishes the sense of distrust which many neighbors still harbor towards Germany. Active U.S. participation in European affairs and good relations with Germany thus contribute decisively to prevent a return to the ill-fated balance-of-power politics of the past.

America needs Europe as well. A Europe that is at peace, prospering, and a reliable partner is of key importance for America's global strategy, which centers on the control of the Eurasian and Asian landmass. It was shortly after September 11, 2001 that former U.S. president George H.W. Bush noted that "just as Pearl Harbor awakened this country from the notion that we could somehow avoid the call to duty and defend freedom in Europe and Asia in World War II, so, too, should this most recent surprise attack erase the concept in some quarters that America can somehow go it alone in the fight against terrorism, or in anything else, for that matter."[24] The U.S. needs partners if it wants to preserve its power in the 21st century (admittedly a view which currently not all U.S. officials would endorse).[25] Likewise, without partners it will not be feasible to fulfill the often-heard demand in the U.S. that the burdens of its international involvement be shared more evenly. The Europeans are the natural partners for the Americans. Despite occasional friction and haggle, the European countries are much closer to the U.S. in terms of politics, culture, religion, and economics than, say, the Asians.

But, unless the Europeans want to be secondary, "junior" partners, they have to "earn" the role of an equal partner. While the U.S. is politically and militarily active almost all over the globe, the EU typically focuses only on Europe and the neighboring regions. The defense of the West's common interests, which include securing access to the oil reserves in the Middle East and keeping open international shipping lanes, to name but two, is by and large left to the U.S. Furthermore, it has not gone unnoticed in Washington that, bar a few exceptions, the Europeans' defense rhetoric is so far not matched by a willingness to invest in the modernization of their militaries.

Here, ESDP can be of significant help because it is an important instrument for enhancing the transatlantic partnership. It is slowly dawning upon Europeans that they will have to do more to defend common Western interests. In order to preserve their worldwide interests, EU members are beginning to acknowledge the need for a sustained political as well as financial and military commitment. Thus, a successful ESDP is in America's interest.

Obviously, there is an inconsistency between the Americans' calls for more effective military contributions and their concerns about diminished political influence in Europe. It should be clear to the U.S., however, that the objective of more capable European forces cannot be separated from the concomitant development of deepening consultation, cooperation and integration. In light of the susceptibility of the international system to crises, the future EU force should be seen as a source of support for NATO, thus adding value to the transatlantic relationship. There is no reason for Washington to be concerned about an EU caucus in NATO since the many "atlanticist" EU members will make sure that America's voice is always heard and its advice heeded.[26]

Moreover, it is quite insightful to compare the U.S.-European security relationship with the relationship in trade, as David Gompert did recently.[27] He points out that, in spite of recurrent disagreement and competing narrow interests, the two great economic powers are in the process of developing a common strategy whose foundation is a common interest in open trade. It is remarkable, he says, that the U.S. welcomes the Europeans' role in the very sphere where "the EU is most assertive on the world stage and, conversely, that the EU's strategy is to complement and encourage, not undercut, U.S. strategy." Gompert concludes that the cooperation in global trade negotiations could be a "prototype of broader partnership to come."

September 11 and Beyond

A balance-sheet of the EU's reaction to, and actions after, September 11 reveals a mixed record. Positive aspects include various initiatives across the EU's different areas and enhanced cooperation with the U.S. in the economic and justice and home affairs sectors. An EU-wide arrest warrant has been introduced. For the CFSP, the struggle against terrorism has become a priority and features prominently in the political dialogues with partner countries, which have been offered support in their fight against terrorism.

On the other hand, the aftermath of September 11 has shown again that, in times of crisis, it is the European nation states and the individual governments, not the high representative for the CFSP, that dominate the political scene. The reactions in the European capitals demonstrated a considerable degree of confusion and disregard for the very person chosen to represent European foreign policy.

The upshot is that the EU has to come up with new, better ideas on how to improve the planning and the implementation of its common foreign policy and how to enhance the position of "Mr. CFSP." Clearly, the principle of semi-annual rotation of the EU presidency has significant disadvantages. Above all, however, EU members need a basic, common understanding of their strategic and foreign policy interests.

Despite some deficiencies, ESDP is the process that will promote the development of such understanding. Events since September 11 have led to increased European involvement, including military operations, in areas and countries as far away as Afghanistan (for the Germans, this would have been unthinkable only ten years ago). The EU knows that it has an obligation—in Europe as well as adjacent regions—to contribute to the stabilization of fragile states because repercussions of their collapse would also be felt in Europe. At the same time, developments since September 11 have underscored the need for a comprehensive approach to crisis management combining both civilian and military tools. Furthermore, Europeans are beginning to acknowledge, albeit slowly, that only a Union which has convincing resources, both political and military, at its disposal will develop into a credible and successful player in international security policy.

One of the next big tests for ESDP might be the response to the Bush administration's emphasis on preemption. Traditionally, deterrence has been the cornerstone of NATO's defense policy. In view of the fact that terrorists are undeterrable, the U.S. focus has shifted to preemptive measures. As a result, many Europeans fear an unrestrained use of force, possibly including nuclear weapons.

More specifically, the issue will be how to deal with Iraq. The U.S. government has declared regime change in Baghdad its goal,[28] and there are several indications that America might be about to embark on a far-reaching strategy aiming at long-term stabilization and democratization of the Middle East.[29] If the first step of this strategy is the deposition of Saddam Hussein's dictatorial regime by force, the EU and its members states will be required to support the U.S. There are mainly two reasons for this. Firstly, the stakes in the Middle East are so high that the EU will by no means be able to leave the tasks of removing Saddam Hussein, destroying his weapons of mass destruction, and establishing a democratic government to the U.S. alone. Hiding behind and objecting to, yet, at the same time, benefiting from America's actions would be no option for the EU.

Secondly, a successful military campaign in Iraq would have to be complemented by a reconstruction of its political structures and society. Here, the EU with its wide range of humanitarian, economic, and civil administration capabilities would be indispensable. Although the Bush 2000 election campaign treated "nation building" and "peacekeeping" as "dirty words" according to Kagan,[30] these are the very tasks Americans would have to engage in together with the Europeans, probably for a long time. If the emerging Middle East strategy of the U.S. is to yield the hoped-for resolution of old conflicts in that region, it will require an effort by the U.S. and Europe similar to the ones America undertook in Japan and Germany after World War II.

Conclusions

The strengthening of a common European security and defense policy has to be seen against the historical background of European integration. Alongside enlargement, economic and monetary union, and the reforms of the EU's institution ESDP is only one of the extraordinary tasks facing the EU. In view of this, the speed with which ESDP has progressed over the past three and a half years is all the more surprising. ESDP is part of a grand ambition to restructure Europe after the end of the Cold War.

Internally, ESDP furthers the development of the EU's external relations structures to meet future security challenges. In view of the differing strategic traditions among EU members and against the background of the CFSP provisions in the TEU, issues such as "when," "where," and "how" to use ESDP mechanisms will nevertheless be difficult to solve at a theoretical level; future crises will play an important role for the development of ESDP.

More generally, ESDP is based on a broad concept of defense that goes beyond the establishment of a corps-sized military force. Particular emphasis is put on the civilian aspects both of crisis prevention and acute crisis management. With its wide range of diplomatic, financial, and economic tools soon to complemented by a rapid reaction force, the EU aspires to offer "one-stop shopping" for crisis management, which will be a first for an international organization. At the strategic level, ESDP seeks to advance the EU's approach of finding common solutions for common problems through multilateral cooperation with all the parties concerned.

Having said that, a lot remains to be done. Europeans are only just beginning to understand that their sense of security is largely due to, not despite, as some have it, the U.S. The threat of being punished by the world's most powerful state has long deterred those who seek to undermine Europe or the West generally. This is changing as new security risks and threats are emerging that have little in common with the old, familiar ones. In order to be able to cope with these shifting security priorities, Europeans need to do more.

EU members have acknowledged that, apart from the many civilian instruments offered by the Union, military capabilities are indispensable for the stabilization and defense of the continent. Military capabilities are also necessary if Europeans want to be listened to on the international stage. Indeed, it is dawning on the European leaders that the defense of the West's common interests requires a due share of European participation. Explaining this to the public and drawing the necessary, albeit painful consequences in all relevant areas, including the cost-intensive armaments sector, would be a major step ahead.

ESDP is still being developed. Many institutional and practical hurdles remain. Although ESDP was declared principally operational in December 2001, the first EU-led mission has yet to be mounted. It will have to be a success lest the project, and probably the EU as a whole, be damaged.

Moreover, two aspects are crucial for the future of ESDP. Firstly, EU member states have to muster the political will to establish a truly *common* foreign and security policy. As the history of European integration shows, European nations are capable of making great strides if these yield benefits for all the participants. There is no doubt that internal and external security can no longer be adequately preserved by the individual nation states. The security challenges of the 21st century have to be met at international level. As a consequence, EU members have to gradually relinquish their diminished national sovereignty in order to gain common sovereignty.

Secondly, in addition to the EU's many civilian tools, ESDP needs to be backed up by real, sufficient military capabilities. The development of the EHG has revealed significant deficiencies in several fields such as strategic mobility and command and control systems. EU member states have made commitments to close these gaps. However, the necessary mechanisms and financial resources have yet to be provided. Europeans will have to make sustained efforts to keep their commitments. Only a Union that is strong economically, politically as well as militarily will evolve into a prominent actor on the world stage.

Such an EU could be America's partner of choice. Occasional differences in opinion notwithstanding, the U.S. and Europe have the same fundamental values and promote peace, prosperity, and freedom in the world. Both sides should protect and defend their common interests together. ESDP is the manifestation of the EU's maturing will to accept its responsibilities.

Notes:

1. Humanitarian, rescue, peacekeeping and peacemaking missions.

2. Joschka Fischer, *From Confederacy to Federation—Thoughts on the Finality of European Integration*, Speech at the Humboldt University, Berlin, 12 May 2000.

3. See Michael Quinlan, *European Defense Cooperation: Asset or Threat to NATO?*, Washington: Woodrow Wilson Center Press, 2001, pp. 1-15 for a concise overview of post-World War II efforts at European defense cooperation.

4. See Michael J. Brenner, *Europe's New Security Vocation*, Institute for National Strategic Studies, National Defense University, Washington, DC, 2002, p. 69 (McNair Paper 66).

5. U.S. Department of Defense, *Strengthening Transatlantic Security: A U.S. Strategy for the 21st Century*, Washington, DC, December 2000, p. 20.

6. Javier Solana, *Europe's Place in the World: The Role of the High Representative*, Stockholm, 25 April 2002.

7. Secretary General/High Representative, *Improving the Coherence and Effectiveness of the European Union Action in the Field of Conflict Prevention*, Report Presented to the Nice European Council, Nice, 7-9 December 2000, paragraph 6.

8. James A. Baker 3d, "A New Europe, A New Atlanticism: Architecture for a New Era," Address to the Berlin Press Club, December 12, 1989, *Vital Speeches of the Day*, January 15, 1990, vol. 56, no. 7, p. 195-199, here: p. 196; and Brenner, *Europe's New Security Vocation*, p. 71.

9. Solana, *Europe's Place in the World*. For the following quotation see ibid.

10. Interestingly, this is also the main point of a little-noticed speech given by Richard N. Haass, director of the policy planning staff at the U.S. State Department. Haas says, "In the 21st century, the principal aim of American foreign policy is to integrate other countries and organizations into arrangements that will sustain a world consistent with U.S. interests and values[.] . . . In this era, our fate is intertwined with the fate of others, so our success must be shared success." He calls this an emerging "Doctrine of Integration." It remains to be seen how prominently Haass' ideas will feature in the Bush administration's foreign policy. See Richard N. Haass, *Defining U.S. Foreign Policy in a Post-Post-Cold War World*, The 2002 Arthur Ross Lecture, Remarks to Foreign Policy Association, New York, NY, 22 April 2002.

11. Javier Solana, *Europe: Security in the Twenty-First Century*, The Olof Palme Memorial Lecture, Stockholm, 20 June 2001, paragraph 27.

12. Romano Prodi, *For a Strong Europe, With a Grand Design And the Means of Action*, Speech at Institut d'Etudes Politiques, Paris, 29 May 2001.

13. Tony Blair, *Speech to the Polish Stock Exchange*, 6 October 2000.

14. See Zbigniew Brzezinski, *The Grand Chessboard: American Primacy and Its Geostrategic Imperatives*, New York: Basic Books, 1997, p. 194f. and Heinrich Buch, Reiner Huber, and Roland Kaestner, "Jenseits der ESVP: Anmerkungen zu einer transatlantischen Strategie," Hans-Georg Ehrhart (ed.), *Die Europäische Sicherheits- und Verteidigungspolitik: Positionen, Perzeptionen, Probleme, Perspektiven*, Baden-Baden: Nomos, 2002, pp. 283-294, here: p. 286f. (Demokratie, Frieden, Sicherheit, vol. 142).

15. Italics added.

16. For a more detailed analysis, see Martin Ortega, *Military Intervention and the European Union*, Institute for Security Studies, Western European Union, Paris, March 2001, p. 101f. (Chaillot Paper 45).

17. See ibid., p. 114f.

18. See Solana, *Europe: Security in the Twenty-First Century*.

19. Bundesnachrichtendienst, *Proliferation von Massenvernichtungsmitteln und Trägerraketen*, October 1999, p. 5 (translation by the author). See also Joseph Cirincione, Jon B. Wolfsthal, and Miriam Rajkumar, *Deadly Arsenals: Tracking Weapons of Mass Destruction*, Washington, D.C.: Carnegie Endowment for International Peace, 2002.

20. See Gerd Föhrenbach, "Die transatlantische Sicherheitspartnerschaft an der Schwelle zum 21. Jahrhundert," *Internationale Politik und Gesellschaft*, no. 1/2001, pp. 40-48.

21. See Javier Solana, *Summary of the Interventions*, Informal Meeting of Defense Ministers, Zaragoza, 22-23 March 2002.

22. Robert Kagan, "Power and Weakness," *Policy Review*, no. 113, June/July 2002, pp. 3-28, here: p. 3.

23. Richard Holbrooke, "America, A European Power," *Foreign Affairs*, vol. 74 (March/April 1995), pp. 38-51.

24. Quoted in: Joseph Nye, "The New Rome Meets the New Barbarians," *The Economist*, 23 March 2002, S. 23-25, here: p. 23.

25. See Daniel Hamilton's chapter in this volume for a more detailed discussion of the different viewpoints in Washington toward Europe and ESDP. See also Nicholas Lemann, "The Bush Administration May Have a Brand-New Doctrine of Power," *The New Yorker*, 25 March 2002 for an insightful analysis of the strategic debate within the Bush administration.

26. See Gerd Föhrenbach, "Security Implications of EU Enlargement," *Baltic Defense Review*, no. 6 (vol. 2001), pp. 7-18.

27. See David C. Gompert, "The EU on the World Stage," *Internationale Politik* (Transatlantic Edition), vol. 3, no. 2, pp. 3-9. For the following quotations see p. 8.

28. See, for example, Richard Cheney, *Speech to Korean War Veterans*, San Antonio, 29 August 2002.

29. See "Saddam and His Sort," *The Economist*, 29 June 2002, Supplement "Present at the Creation," p. 17/18, here: p. 18; and Matthias Rüb, "Washingtons neuer Irak," *Frankfurter Allgemeine Zeitung*, 12 August 2002, p. 3.

30. Robert Kagan, "America Will Have to Stay in Iraq," *International Herald Tribune*, 22 July 2002, p. 8.

ESDP and Enlargement

Sir Michael Quinlan

The biggest project facing the European Union, now that the launch of the single currency is past, is that of enlargement to include a substantial number of new member countries. This enlargement will affect to some degree, and in certain fields radically, every facet of the Union's business. ESDP will be no exception. Can we identify what the impact on ESDP will be, so as to be ready to cope with it when it comes, to exploit its beneficial aspects and lighten any less welcome ones? And can we also identify, conversely, what the impact of the ESDP project may be upon new members themselves? We need to take into account also that the North Atlantic Alliance will be undertaking its own enlargement, with overlapping coverage.

The Present Scene

The Union currently has fifteen members. It has not attempted to define its eventual geographical boundaries. It has not, for example, said anything that would permanently exclude states that were once, like Ukraine, part of the original Soviet Union. Its intended qualifying limits have been expressed in terms of the character of states—stable democracy, free-market economic system, respect for human rights, readiness to accept the Union's *acquis*—rather than their location. Some of the further reaches of conceivable expansion could raise significant new issues and challenges in the field of foreign policy and security. We may however reasonably focus the present analysis upon states officially recognised by the Union as candidates for membership.

There are thirteen such applicant states. They are widely different in size (Poland will rank equal with Spain as having the Unions fifth-largest population; Malta's is less than Luxembourg's) and diverse in character, though ten of them share the burden of a recent Communist history. In alphabetical order, they are Bulgaria, Cyprus, the Czech Republic, Estonia, Hungary, Latvia, Lithuania, Malta, Poland, Romania, Slovakia, Slovenia and Turkey. Substantive accession negotiations are in progress with twelve of these; the exception is Turkey, on grounds that the political conditions are not yet dependably met there. The EU summit at Nice in December 2000 declared an intention to complete the negotiations by the end of 2002 for all applicants regarded as meeting the basic conditions, with a view to membership becoming effective in mid-2004, in time for new members to take part in the elections then due for the European Parliament. Ten of the twelve under-negotiation applicants are regarded as prospective entrants on this timetable, though entry would not have to be simultaneous for all ten; the pace is not to be set by the slowest. The exceptions to the 2004 possibility are Bulgaria and Romania, not expected to be fully ready for membership before 2007.

Evaluation of the effect of enlargement upon ESDP can reasonably concentrate at present upon the twelve. Turkey's accession stands to have greater long-term impact than that of any among these; but it is not realistically to be expected for another decade, and it is unfruitful to attempt now to assess in any detail what the context will then be.

The precise timescale of the first batch of accessions is not yet beyond doubt. The date cannot for any of them be any earlier than the "Nice" target of mid-2004, but it could slip beyond that, for example if at the end of 2002 there remain unresolved severe enlargement-related disagreements—especially over agriculture and structural funds—both among existing members and between them and several of the applicants.

ESDP is part of the EU "package" which new members will automatically take on unless they specifically declare (as Denmark alone among present members has done) that they wish to stand apart from it. None has indicated any such intent, even though none has evident reason to feel special zest for ESDP.

When they join, they will not find that ESDP takes them into wholly unfamiliar fields of cooperation in Western military business. Three of them—the Czech Republic, Hungary and Poland—have been members of NATO since 1999. Almost all have been for several years members of NATO's Partnership for Peace program. They have moreover had significant experience, generally perceived as constructive, of working with the forces of existing EU members in the course of peacekeeping efforts in the Balkans. That experience will have been under NATO and not EU auspices, but since the EU intends to operate ESDP by NATO standards and procedures the experience is relevant.

In addition to that, the EU has from ESDP's inception, in accordance with the "no-discrimination" principle which it declared (and which then U.S. Secretary of State Madeleine Albright underscored), sought to involve European non-members in the ESDP enterprise. All the applicant states were among those invited to attend the EU's Capabilities Commitment Conference in November 2000 and the follow-up Capabilities Improvement Conference a year later; and all made promises of contribution in one form or another (though these were not counted towards the quantified Headline Goals which the Union's December 1999 Helsinki summit had laid down).

The applicant countries have also been included in the institutional arrangements for managing ESDP developed by the Union during 2000 and 2001. These arrangements make provision for systematic dialogue between existing members and the applicants (as well as with non-EU non-applicant European members of NATO) about the development and use of ESDP. The arrangements have as yet been little exercised, but the reason for that lies not in hesitations among or about the applicants but in the general hiatus imposed upon important aspects of ESDP development by the Greece/Turkey problem noted on page 30 below.

Uncertainties and Prospects

The ESDP into whose full management new Union members will be drawn from 2004 onwards is itself as yet by no means mature, nor is its environment static. We cannot hope meaningfully to consider the impact of their arrival in isolation from the uncertainties which bear upon ESDP now or in early prospect. Some of these uncertainties are internal to the project itself; others relate to its wider setting. A current list might include (and even then almost inevitably fail to be exhaustive) the following:

    a. The persistent impasse over developing and defining the "Berlin-plus" arrangements for EU access to NATO assets.

    b. Remaining issues about the conduct of force planning for ESDP and its relationship to NATO processes.

c. Decisions taken, and experience undergone, in any practical application of ESDP that the EU may choose to take on in the near future, the most evident candidate being the monitoring task in the Former Yugoslav Republic of Macedonia.

d. The degree of achievement reached in meeting the Helsinki Headline Goals.

e. The adequacy or otherwise of defense budget provision in EU countries.

f. Any arrangements made for multinational provision of elements of ESDP capability, and perhaps for common financing.

g. The scope of expansion to NATO membership emerging from NATO's prospective meeting of Heads of Government in Prague in November 2002.

h. Any substantial re-casting, at the Prague summit, of NATO's future role and the requirements it sets.

i. The possible impact of the European Convention led by Valéry Giscard d'Estaing on the general working (and the collective political outlook and morale) of the Union.

j. The condition of U.S.-EU relations, both generally and on specific security-related issues like the International Criminal Court; above all, and perhaps massively repercussive, over what happens about the problem dealing with Saddam Hussein's Iraq.

Beyond all these particular questions there lies a general uncertainty of a different but not less important character. The political attention of government leaders is a finite commodity, as are their energy, enthusiasm and willingness to incur domestic political costs. It is already hard to avoid the judgment that resources of these kinds have been deployed more sparingly in support of ESDP in the last two years than they were in its initial formative period after the France/UK meeting at St. Malo in December 1998 and the EU's Cologne summit which formally launched ESDP in June 1999. Competing demands seem unlikely to grow any less pressing over the next two years, as the resolution of the problems of enlargement itself and the handling of the outcome of the Giscard Convention's work dominate the internal agenda.

Against this fluid background, we might consider the impact of enlargement upon ESDP in relation to capabilities; to institutions and methods; and to actual use.

Capabilities

At first glance it may seem obvious that the accession of ten new states, with a further two to follow, must entail a valuable addition to ESDP capability. That is indeed potentially so; but a number of qualifications need to be considered.

The ten first-wave applicants have at present a total of about 370,000 military personnel listed as on active duty. Bulgaria and Romania have a further 180,000. (For comparative scale, the fourteen present EU members engaged in ESDP—that is, excluding Denmark—have about 1.6 million.) Such figures however give little indication of capability available for the tasks to which ESDP is directed. The great bulk of all these numbers comprise personnel— including many conscripts on relatively short-term service—who are not equipped, trained, organised or politically available for complex or sensitive assignments outside their own homelands. Qualitatively inadequate or incompatible contingents would be a drag upon, not an enhancement to, collective ESDP capability.

The fact that, as noted earlier, all the applicants had already made offers of contribution at the EU's capability conferences in 2000 and 2001 means moreover that the net increment on accession is not nec- essarily substantial. It is however likely that membership of the Union will render such offers more lastingly dependable, and in addition make it more likely that the offering countries will be willing to develop their contributions, on a long-term basis, in ways that max- imise their practical value-adding effect within the ESDP framework.

Such development may be especially important for the smaller countries which form the majority. It is impossible for them to field anything approaching a full range of military capabilities to modern and deployable standards in viable amounts; but it should be feasible for them to provide "niche" capabilities of a specialist kind that would fit into wider effort on a pre-arranged basis and to common stan- dards—medical-service teams, for example, or particular categories of logistic support, or even (especially in respect of Cyprus, and perhaps

Malta) making prepared base facilities available to support ESDP deployments. At the same time, it would need to be recognised that contributions of this kind, if they were to be reliable enough to bear weight, would imply a degree of expected if not formal political commitment not to stand aside from common effort as contingencies arose. It might also be desirable that specialist contributions should not be exclusively of a kind that left risky in-harm's-way effort entirely to others.

The identification and design of military contribution to ESDP from the applicant countries will need—as that of existing EU members already does—to be aligned as closely as possible with what NATO too is asking for. It is likely that the Prague summit will see a renewal—and perhaps a better-prioritised re-focusing—of the Defense Capabilities Initiative launched at the Alliance's 1999 Washington summit. NATO is the acknowledged standard-setter in most aspects of equipment characteristics, procedures, organisation and doctrine. In addition, eleven—including the largest five—of the EU's fifteen current members are members also of NATO; and of the twelve under-negotiation applicants for the EU three are already NATO members and at least a further five, and possibly seven, will probably be accepted into NATO at the Prague meeting. It must be likely that in the long run the convergence of European membership between the Union and the North Atlantic Alliance will grow steadily closer.

It is to be expected that EU countries will increasingly face awkward decisions about where to procure the major equipment needed for improved capability—whether within Europe, perhaps on a better-coordinated basis than in the past, or from the United States. The A400M heavy-lift aircraft project is an early illustration—not altogether encouraging, as some would hold—of the problem. The debate on this large and difficult issue is by no means yet fully joined among existing EU members. It seems unlikely that applicant countries will play any large part in its evolution, though given that none of them (except possibly, in the long run, Poland) is likely to be a big defense-industrial player it might be thought that they would regard themselves as free to give priority to the advantages, usually, of U.S. sourcing in value for money and NATO inter-operability. But no doubt political pressures to the contrary would be brought to bear by some other EU members.

Bringing even a small proportion of total active forces among the EU applicants up to NATO or ESDP standards, and re-shaping or re-orienting them to fit optimally within the wider collective effort, will not be a swift undertaking; and it will not be cost-free. The majority of the twelve have defense budgets falling, in terms of percentage of gross domestic product, below even the modest level of the current membership, and mostly with economies still, in varying degree, in post-Communist recovery. Like several existing EU members they will not find it easy, amid domestic pressures, to carry through reform of current military structures in ways, or on a scale, that would release substantial resources for the benefit of ESDP. Whether the fact of entry into the Union and consequent full participation in ESDP will generate a stimulus to greater defense effort, or by contrast tempt governments to relax as they cease to be suppliants, may depend upon outside factors such as the political example set by existing EU members (with Germany at present not an encouraging model in this regard) and also on whether the eventual economic terms of the wider enlargement deal reached for each of them eases or intensifies the strain upon government spending.

Beyond all this, moreover, nature has created a new demand upon the financial resources of both some of the applicants and some existing EU members. The need to make good the widespread and severe damage caused across Central Europe by the exceptional floods of summer 2002 is imposing unexpected and urgent bills of massive size—certainly running in aggregate to many billions of dollars—upon Austria, the Czech Republic, Germany, Hungary and Poland. The role of armed-forces personnel in helping to deal with the calamity has won them favorable public attention; but it can scarcely be assumed that this approval will be reflected in defense-budget increases. There are indeed already instances of the disaster's being made the reason, or at least the pretext, for cutback of defense procurement plans.

Institutions and Methods

The EU's drive to complete the institutional development of ESDP is still partly mired in two internal disputes. The less severe of these concerns the relationship between ESDP force planning processes (not operational planning ones—it is broadly agreed that these should rest with NATO staffs for any large operation) and NATO's long -

established force planning system accompanied now, for willing non-NATO countries, by the Partnership Analysis and Review Process. The inclination of a few members towards emphasising detached EU independence remains in some degree at odds with the preference of the majority for avoiding duplication. The graver dispute however concerns the question of Turkey's association with the workings of ESDP. For three years now there has been disagreement about the terms that should govern this, with the point of impasse alternating between Ankara and Athens. The problem continues damagingly to block the proper completion of arrangements, under the "Berlin-plus" concept, for ESDP operations to have access to NATO assets.

It must be likely that in both these disputes the general inclination of the applicants (save no doubt Cyprus, as virtually Greece's client) would, if put to the test, converge with whatever is acceptable to the majority of present members. Almost all of them see membership in the EU, like that in NATO, as part of their re-incorporation into the wider West, and their prime instinct in such matters will be consensual and Atlanticist. But it is earnestly to be hoped that in respect of both disputes this can remain matter for historical speculation. Though the way forward in the disputes is unclear at this writing, for them to be still unsettled as late as mid-2004, when applicants may first join the Union, would imply that the ESDP project was in serious political difficulty.

As regards other aspects of ESDP's structural evolution, the applicant countries would probably be found alongside those (like Germany) who favour a wider use of multilateral provision and common financing of capabilities, rather than those (like the United Kingdom) whose preference is mostly more restrictive and nation-based. But it would anyway be wrong to suppose that joint provision would necessarily entail significant resource transfers to poorer countries in relief of the budgetary pressures reviewed on page 29; its likely aim would be efficiency and equitable spread, not cross-subsidy.

The addition of the applicant countries, increasing the number around the table on ESDP business from fifteen to twenty-five and then twenty-seven, is bound to carry with it some increase in administrative costs and probably also some inflation of central personnel numbers, for example in the EU Military Staff, as new members seek representation. It seems unlikely that the outcome of the European

Convention will have much direct impact upon decision-making in the military field. The Convention has set up a working party to examine ESDP-related questions; but whatever it may recommend, this is the field where nations are least apt to surrender control to either majority vote or supra-national authority.

Whether the expansion has a damaging effect upon the complexity of business and the speed with which it is transacted will depend in part upon how quickly new members master working style and conventions, and on whether they judge it important to present to their colleagues a carefully cooperative aspect; most of them, surely, would so judge. There would almost inevitably be a particular learning period, and perhaps some awkward adaptation, in absorbing the new members into the arrangements for the secure handling of intelligence material and other sensitive inputs. It is to be hoped that this could be managed without intensifying problems in relations with United States authorities in this field, where ready interchange between the EU and NATO is especially important.

The Use of ESDP Capability

The most interesting questions—but also the hardest to answer at all confidently—about the impact of enlargement upon ESDP relate to how the accession of new members may influence EU decisions about whether, where and how to put collective military capability to operational use.

In formal terms use of the capability, as being an inter-governmental and not a supra-national European Commission matter, requires unanimity among all member nations—that is, positive assent or at least the absence of objection from each. From that standpoint, the need to involve twenty-five and later twenty-seven countries instead of the present fifteen looks calculated to enhance braking rather than propulsive power. But political working is often more pragmatic and less tidy than that would imply. Just for example, an isolated objector might find it harder to stand out against a more numerous and more diverse near-consensus.

The likely instinctive attitudes of the applicant countries to the use of their military forces in action abroad cannot be easily summarised or aggregated. National experiences differ considerably between one and another. None of them is habituated to undertaking foreign intervention in the way that France and the United Kingdom have been. Almost all save the smallest have however been willing, since the break-up of the Soviet Union and the Warsaw Pact, to contribute to tasks in the Balkans and sometimes elsewhere; and none of them is especially scarred by bad experiences of the Srebrenica or Somalia kind.

It may reasonably be expected that their general inclination, as having more to prove than members already established, will be to show themselves positive partners in enterprises where the Union manages to give reality to the concept of common foreign and security policy; and most of them may have fewer hang-ups about the idea of using military force than some current members. They may also be among those more disposed towards a forward EU role in United Nations-initiated tasks, at least where the scale of commitment required is modest.

It has been noted earlier that their outlook is more likely to be Atlanticist than Gaullist. If that proves so, they will tend to side with those EU members who prefer to see ESDP, in respect of both capability and deployment, as primarily a reinforcement of the EU's weight in partnership with the United States in the maintenance of international order rather than a manifestation of separate and preferred independence in action. ESDP's maturing and shaping in such respects is however more likely anyway to be driven by the unforecastable pressures of specific crises than by doctrinal disposition beforehand. And there looms above all these speculations, for both present and future EU members, the huge and crucial unknown (at this writing) of what is done about the Saddam Hussein regime in Iraq, and how that Middle Eastern drama plays out. The potential impact upon both the transatlantic relationship and EU cohesion in external policy, and so upon ESDP and much else, can scarcely be overrated.

Another dimension of possible attitude among the aspirants is the geographical one. For most of them, the prime natural focus of external security interest and concern lies to the East rather than—as now for most existing members who have outward-looking inclinations at all—towards the Mediterranean basin, in the Middle East and in the deep problems of sub-Saharan Africa. The weight of Russia means that if problems posing a possible need for military force do arise in the East they will tend to look to NATO, as bringing in the United States, rather than the EU and ESDP. That apart, however, they may be minded to side with those current members chary of avoidable heavy involvement southward or further afield where critics can characterise the tasks as of a post-colonial character.

Will enlargement make any marked difference to the EU's general political weight in the world, to how it sees itself as a participant in global security tasks, and to what its own people expect of it in such tasks? Here too the prospect is cloudy. The enlarged Union will comprise a significantly larger proportion of UN membership; it will be of considerably broader geographical extent, and with new and wider boundary interfaces, sometimes with neighbors of imperfect stability. But even when all twelve have joined the increment will be less marked in population (at about twenty-eight per cent) and in gross domestic product (at barely five per cent) than in membership count. Internal problems will in several respects become more demanding, and the sheer number of sovereign participants risks creating a more muscle-bound collectivity. The EU is inherently by no means inward-looking, as the scale of its effort in external development and humanitarian aid testifies (see Bruno Tertrais' discussion in chapter 8, p. 118); but a heavy and awkward internal agenda might tempt it towards an unambitious view of opportunities and responsibilities in the relatively new field of involvement in the military aspects of international security. Robust, skilful and cohesive leadership will be needed from the larger existing members if aspirations for the Union to be a bigger player in that field are to be realised.

ESDP and Multilateral Security Organizations: Working with NATO, the UN and OSCE

Marc Otte*

The European security scene has a distinct character that places it apart among other regions of the world. It is unique for the high degree of institutionalization among international players on the continent and the central importance of the transatlantic link. This special relationship finds its roots in a community of interests and, more deeply, in a shared model of civilization, what Felipe Fernandes Armesto calls the Atlantic Ocean civilization.[1]

This dense grid of institutions has provided and continues to provide a framework for co-operation and integration among nation states interested in European security, in the pursuit of the stability and the security of their common space. This chapter will examine the impact of the European Security and Defense Policy on the region's institutions.

The Institutions

NATO remains the cornerstone of collective defense and has become the main player in military crisis management and cooperative security in the post Cold War period. The OSCE has built on the principles of the CSCE to become a pan-European collective security umbrella for the vast Euro-Atlantic area, "from Vancouver to Vladivostok." The European Union has been a comprehensive enterprise of stability through economic integration that is well on the way to include almost all the states of the continent. It has more recently embarked on a process to also become a strategic actor on the world scene, including the capacity to act militarily. The Council of Europe, although a more discreet institution, has its place in this concert of

---

*Mr. Otte writes in his personal capacity. The views represented are his and do not necessarily represent the views of the General Secretariat of the Council of the European Union.

organizations. By promoting the practice of human rights, pluralist democracy and the rule of law, as well as awareness and development of Europe's cultural identity among its members, it plays a "civilizing" role that contributes to a form of "societal security" across Europe.

The founding charters of these institutions refer to common values and principles. They explicitly commit their members to the respect of the UN Charter.[2] Together, they constitute the most sophisticated functioning model in the world to replace, on a regional basis, a system of international relations based purely on the balance of power principles, by a rule-based system exploiting the benefits of interdependence, furthering co-operation among the actors and instituting codes of conduct among them. They have developed mechanisms of consultation that increase the predictability of the behavior of the players concerned and facilitate the peaceful resolution of conflicts. They also have progressively put in place more effective instruments to prevent and manage crises.

The EU and NATO have promoted from the start various degrees of integration among member states, as a further incentive to deepening solidarity and avoiding the return of conflicts originating in historical antagonisms and grievances. In the case of NATO, the integrated military structure prevented the re-nationalization of defense policies and the forming of changing ad hoc military coalitions.

Defense was part of the first attempts at European integration, but the circumstances of the Cold War redirected energies in the European Community towards economic integration. This led to an informal work sharing arrangement with NATO during the Cold War under which the latter ensured collective defense and the European institutions that came into existence on the foundations of the Rome Treaty, provided a security foundation through economic and social reconstruction and progressive prosperity.

Even during the Cold War, co-operation did not remain limited to the Western countries. The concept of détente and the doctrine of peaceful coexistence opened the way for an institutionalized relationship between East and West. The Conference for Security and Co-operation in Europe initiated a long, gradual process of co-operation between all parties interested in European security, encompassing already at that time all the dimensions of security: military, economic and human rights. From international conference, the CSCE gradually developed more permanent features and would in the end become the OSCE.

After the fall of the Berlin wall, there was a period of uncertainty. Some predicted that the dissolution of the Warsaw Pact would take NATO down the same path. The potential reunification of the European continent would call for a pan-European collective security organization, on the foundations laid by the CSCE.

The crises and conflicts resulting from the break-up of the former Yugoslavia invalidated this prognosis. They underlined the lack of cohesion of the EU, resulting in the inefficiency of the WEU, which had become, since the Maastricht treaty, the military instrument of the EU. They demonstrated the inability of the OSCE to manage crises of any significant dimension. They also shed a harsh light on the inadequacy of the peacekeeping concepts developed at the UN during the Cold War. After the U.S. decision to be engaged in the Balkans, NATO turned out to be the only organization capable to plan and manage effectively a new form of intervention of the international community in a local conflict. Only NATO proved able to send a credible military force, with a mandate robust enough to stop hostilities and dissuade the belligerents to restart their conflicts, thereby creating a security environment within which civilian organizations could initiate a process of peace building and reconstruction.

These developments had important consequences for the future of Euro-Atlantic institutions and for their mutual relations, as well as for their interactions with the UN system.

They also gave rise to various—and sometimes competing—concepts about the global architecture of European security after the Cold War. One was the notion of "interlocking institutions," which would combine their strengths and mutually reinforce their actions, in support of the reunification and the stabilization of the European continent, associating Russia and the United States. Their respective memberships reach far beyond the traditional view of the geographical expanse of Europe, encompassing the former Soviet republics of Central Asia and the Caucasus. In the context of the new OSCE, such a vision included in fact the entire Euro-Atlantic area, "from Vancouver to Vladivostok." The Clinton administration had articulated its own vision of the institutional support for this new architecture under the "Triple Crown" concept. According to this model, three main institutional umbrellas were supposed to implement the new European architecture. NATO would ensure security, the EU prosperity and the OSCE democracy. This presentation was first developed for domestic consumption and in particular, to secure support of the U.S. Congress for the Administration's design for post Cold War Europe and further U.S. engagement in Europe. But it reflected of course a real political agenda for the future of transatlantic relations and was indicative of the way the administration intended to retool the available institutional instruments. It provided a template for the future tasks of the transatlantic partnership. Europe and the U.S. would work together to complete the unification of Europe and to firmly anchor Russia in the West. But the concept was also part of a wider ambition to lay the basis for a partnership beyond the confines of Europe, where the future main challenges were bound to arise.

At the same time, the EU was well under way in completing a single market and setting in motion a timetable towards a single currency. These two steps meant a significant qualitative progress of the integration process, pushing the EU further away from the intergovernmental character of other international institutions and increasing the solidarity among member states towards new forms of supranational governance. Together with the historic duty to open membership to the new democracies of Central and Eastern Europe, these developments were a strong incentive to make more decisive progress in strengthening the political dimension of European integration, which had always been part of the vision of the Founding Fathers. A more effective foreign and security policy was seen as an essential element of this project. Its principles were defined in the Maastricht and Amsterdam treaties. The basic aim was to equip the EU with the means to safeguard the continuation of European integration, to defend its vital interests and promote its model in the world at large. The lessons of the Balkans crises had underlined the necessity to strengthen the security component of European external action and in particular the autonomous capacity to act militarily. This meant a potential big qualitative step in the Common Foreign and Security Policy. The successful completion of that project would mean that Europe would go beyond the "soft power" approach that had been the hallmark of its external policies so far. By taking the EU out of its economic box the new European Security and Defense Policy embodies the ambition to make it a global player, able to apply the whole range of instruments of action in the international arena. ("a superpower but not a superstate," in the words of British Prime Minister Tony Blair.)

The implementation of this ambition in the field of defense became at first a bone of contention with the U.S., where the vision of a European security and defense identity was still seen as embedded in NATO, according to the parameters of the NATO Berlin ministerial meeting in 1996 that defined the parameters of an European Security and Defense Identity within the framework of NATO. Any move of the EU towards a more autonomous course in defense and military matters raised the fear of loosening transatlantic solidarity and weakening NATO. It led to the warning from the U.S. Secretary of State, Madeleine Albright, about the three "D's" ("no duplication, no discrimination, no decoupling").

The demise of the Soviet Empire and the domestic turmoil in Russia meant a significant weakening of this country on the world stage and in Europe in particular. An initial co-operative attitude on the part of Moscow evolved gradually into a more negative and confrontational stance. Unable to enforce its perceived security interests with respect to the Balkans and to NATO, and to a lesser extent, EU enlargement, Russia adopted a strategy designed to put obstacles where it could in the path of NATO preponderance. It promoted an alternative institutional design: the strengthening of the OSCE as the overall collective security organization in Europe. It sought the adoption of a new charter for European security that would give the OSCE a pre-eminent role in mandating and managing crises in Europe, under the authority of the UNSC. That project included the development of military structures enabling the OSCE to lead military peacekeeping operations and ensure their political control. This ambition still exists today in the Russian vision, as demonstrated by recent proposals tabled by the Russian delegation in Vienna.

Institutions are not ends in themselves. Their role is ultimately decided first by the nature of their membership, the political agenda of the dominant players and the political will and resources member states make available to them. The capacity they demonstrate to react at any given moment to unfolding events and to adapt to changing strategic circumstances is a second major factor. In the period following the Cold War, it became evident that the nature of security risks had changed dramatically. The existential threat to physical survival had given way to a range of more or less serious interrelated threats and challenges, combining lack of development and growing economic disparities, uncontrolled migrations, environmental hazards, health risks, identity crises and ethnic conflicts. These situations have created a fertile ground for terrorism and proliferation of weapons of mass destruction. The feeling of insecurity has grown more personal. Separating internal and external security is becoming artificial. Within the framework of an increasingly globalized international system these new security conditions have favored the emergence of a range of strategic non-state actors on the international scene. These include powerful NGO's, terrorist and criminal organizations and a host of transnational networks, all pursuing their own agendas, good or bad, but increasingly out of the control of individual governments. International media are also fast becoming independent players, setting priorities as to what event or which part of the world deserves the attention of public opinion and policy makers. Information strategies have become central preoccupations for security organizations.

The ability of international organizations to confront the new threats and to deal effectively with the new players has had a strong influence on their relevance in the post Cold War era.

The Balkan experience

For all the international institutions concerned, the Balkans wars have been a defining moment.

NATO

NATO found a new lease of life thanks to its unique ability to deliver the appropriate military response to the Balkan wars and to the readiness of the U.S., after some hesitation, to use its military and diplomatic weight in the new European crises. This opened the way for a transformation of the Alliance. It adopted a new Strategic Concept, empowering it to act out of area and to engage in "non-Article 5" or military crisis management missions, opened the door for enlargement to new members and engaged into an adaptation of its military structures in order to execute its new military missions. Through the Partnership for Peace and the Euro-Atlantic Partnership Council, it has put in place a vast network of co-operative security, encompassing almost all the membership of the OSCE. While retaining its collective defense function, it became the main actor for co-operative security in the politico- military field and for co-operation in military crisis management in the whole Euro-Atlantic area. Its comparative advantage in that respect remains anchored in the unchallenged American military power and U.S. leadership in NATO.

European Union

The Balkan crises were also central for the EU. They constituted a wake-up call for European leaders by making obvious the lack of political will and of cohesion in foreign policy, the deficiencies of its decision-making procedures and the weakness of European military capabilities. These shortcomings prevented Europe to take the central role it should have been playing in stopping war and humanitarian disasters in its own backyard. The initial hesitations of the U.S. to intervene constituted a warning that the U.S. might no longer be automatically involved in all European crises and underlined the necessity for Europeans to take a bigger share of their own security. It was a further incentive to rapidly develop the capacity to decide and to act, on the basis of credible military capabilities, when the NATO option would not be available. At the same time, its potential to muster and use effectively a very wide range of policy instruments under the same political roof, gave the EU a definite edge in the ability to manage a crisis across its whole spectrum, including in the area of conflict prevention, both in a long and a short term perspective. Its own model of integration is the most powerful tool for conflict prevention. On the European continent, it can offer membership as the ultimate incentive to civilized behavior and good governance. It offers the best guarantee against instability. Outside Europe, the EU strives to promote its model and has done so through a range of instruments, such as the Barcelona process with its Mediterranean partners and the deepening cooperation with regional organizations like ASEAN and MERCOSUR.

OSCE

The OSCE never became a significant player in military crisis management or a leading political organization. The majority of its member states did not favor such a development; and have prevented the OSCE from building up the necessary structures and obtaining resources to play such a role. On the other hand, the organization has acquired a strong profile in the area of standards setting and as an instrument of early warning, conflict prevention and post-conflict rehabilitation. It has become a respected watchdog and effective facilitator for the improvement of human rights and of the rights of minorities. It has acquired an indispensable role in democracy building.

Its efficiency is based on its flexibility and on the presence of its field missions in areas of conflicts, where they represent in many cases the only link to the external world and sole official presence of the international community. The OSCE also constitutes a useful framework to include all the countries that have no prospect of EU or NATO membership for the foreseeable future, in the pursuit of a broad security agenda and common standards of governance in the whole Euro-Atlantic area. It remains the forum where efficient tools for confidence building measures and arms control continue to be developed. The adaptation of the treaty on limitations of conventional forces in Europe (CFE), was concluded under its auspices and constitutes a major achievement in the post-Cold War period, although its ratification has been put on hold by Russia in relation to the issue of the likely Baltic states accession to NATO. The vast range of confidence building and verification instruments and concepts, developed within OSCE, has become a reference for other regional security regimes.

United Nations

The Balkan experience, along with the genocide in Rwanda, highlighted the basic flaws of UN peacekeeping in the kind of violent conflicts that became the hallmark of the post Cold War period. The ensuing soul-searching led to the publication of the Brahimi report and to closer consultations with NATO, the EU and the OSCE in drawing the lessons of recent failures and shortcomings. The deeper involvement of Euro-Atlantic institutions in the management of crises and the capabilities they developed to that effect became the subject of intense interest by the UN. It fitted the trend towards devolution of implementation of UN peacekeeping mandates to relevant regional organizations. Europe was the obvious place to start, given its high degree of institutionalization in the security field. The increased involvement of European and Euro-Atlantic organizations in crisis management, conflict prevention and peacekeeping was also seen as a hopeful sign for a reversal of a trend that indicated a gradual disengagement of the Western countries from UN peacekeeping. This evolution raised expectations for the timely and efficient implementation of the main operational conclusions of the Brahimi report, in particular the strengthening of the support structures for peacekeeping, the improvement of the efficiency of decision making, planning and action.

ESDP in particular was seen as a way of bolstering the credibility and the capacities for UN crisis management, in terms of financial and political support but also in terms of much needed military and civilian crisis management capacities for UN peace operations. It would potentially improve the availability to the UN of a set of forces properly trained, structured and equipped as well as interoperable, able to intervene quickly and efficiently. In view of traditional European positions concerning the role of the UN, it also provided assurances that ESDP would preserve the place of the UN as universal reference for mandates and legitimacy. Public statements of European leaders in that sense confirmed this expectation. Furthermore, it opened new opportunities to promote the EU model of regional integration as a reference for other regions in the world and the development or strengthening of other regional institutions.

ESDP and co-operation with the UN, NATO and OSCE

The Balkan crises were also a testing ground for the co-operation between the UN and European organizations. It was a learning process. The early years were not very positive. The UN, NATO, and the EU worked competitively for a time, often canceling out efforts to bring peace in Bosnia and Croatia. Lack of knowledge of respective procedures and diverging political agendas were the prime reasons for this situation.

Principles and modalities for more efficient co-operation emerged from practice and much of what has been codified to this day is the result of lessons learned in the field. The adoption of the principles and modalities of co-operation with international organizations in the framework of ESDP owes a lot to this field experience.

The guiding principles adopted in successive EU policy documents are added value, interoperability, and visibility of EU contributions and autonomy of decision making of the EU. Principles and modalities include:

- A pragmatic and flexible approach. In each case the aim is to focus on substance and concrete needs for increased co-operation.

- A dialogue on lessons learned from field experience and on best practice, which forms the basis for the developments of common standards in terms of training of personnel and operational concepts.

- Provisions for regular contacts between the political bodies of the respective interlocutors and between their international secretariats.

- Practical co-operation between their crisis management structures, during and outside times of crisis.

- Evolutionary nature, in function of further developments of ESDP.

- The perspective of an integrated approach to crisis management. For this reason the EU is also pursuing coherence between the co-operation principles and modalities adopted with each institution.

EU-NATO

Co-operation with NATO is an organic component of ESDP. Two founding principles of ESDP are that the EU would act militarily where NATO as whole is not engaged and that it would not create unnecessary duplications. The declared aim of EU-NATO co-operation is that of a strategic partnership. EU and NATO have agreed on and are implementing principles and modalities for regular consultations between their respective councils and international secretariats. They have also agreed on the need for co-operation in the field of capability development and improvement.

The guiding principles for EU-NATO co-operation in times of crisis have been set in the so-called "Berlin plus" arrangement. The NATO ministerial Berlin decision in 1996 was designed to build an effective European pillar in NATO. Its goal was to facilitate the release of NATO assets and capabilities for operations led by the Europeans (at the time in the framework of the Western European Union), including the identification of command arrangements that would be separable but not separate from the NATO military structures. The concept of CJTF (Combined Joint Task Forces), specific command arrangements for crisis management or non-article 5 missions, was adopted in this context.

The Western European Union (WEU) and NATO subsequently negotiated framework arrangements for WEU access to NATO assets and capabilities. The distinction between the two terms had the following rationale: whereas assets (defined as personnel, headquarters, headquarters elements, units and equipment) were transferred to the control of WEU, capabilities (defined as services such as airborne early warning, information, access to communications, etc.) remained under NATO control.

The so-called "Berlin plus" project was designed to take account of the evolution that had taken place since the development of ESDP in the EU, which had decided to take over the crisis management functions of the WEU. The Washington Summit identified four areas for implementation of "Berlin plus" in paragraph 10 of the Washington Summit Communiqué:

a. Assured EU access to NATO planning capabilities able to contribute to military planning for EU-led operations;

b. The presumption of availability to the EU of pre-identified NATO capabilities and common assets for use in EU-led operations;

c. Identification of a range of European command options for EU-led operations, further developing the role of DSACEUR in order for him to assume fully and effectively his European responsibilities;

    d. The further adaptation of NATO's defense planning system to incorporate more comprehensively the availability of forces for EU-led operations.[3]

The crucial innovation is the assured access to NATO planning capabilities and the presumption of availability of pre-identified NATO capabilities and common assets. It is a major guarantee against duplication and in favor of a strong partnership in military crisis management. Its essential feature is to give the EU a high degree of confidence that NATO assets and capabilities would be available for EU-led operations, should the EU choose to have recourse to them.

The implementation of Berlin plus, will require a lot of work. The level of availability and nature of decision to be taken will vary according to the type of assets and capabilities. "Assured access" applies to the planning machinery of NATO, essentially for operational planning, on the basis of an EU request. Presumption of availability of pre-identified assets and capabilities could in principle only apply to NATO collective and common assets. The decision to release these assets and capabilities would be taken by NATO, evidently on a case-by-case basis, because NATO would never be able to give assurances in advance that they are available at the time of an EU request. But a sort of confirmatory mechanism could be sought thanks to which the EU would be able to take for granted that assets and capabilities would be available unless advised otherwise. Examples in this category are CJTF and other Command Structure HQ's, deployable command and control equipment, airborne early warning (AWACS), pipelines and provision of intelligence/information. National assets and capabilities for an EU-led operation would of course be dependent on a national decision by the nation concerned, evidently also on a case by case basis. The EU response to the NATO offer for access to its assets and capabilities is contained in the provisions adopted at the European Council at Nice for EU-NATO co-operation in crisis management. [4]

In order to get agreement on these principles and modalities, the related issue of the participation of non-EU European NATO allies and European candidates to EU accession had to be solved. After long and intensive discussions all NATO allies have agreed on the principles and modalities for participation except one. Turkey still believes that the EU offer does not take its security interests and its contribution to European security sufficiently into account. Intense diplomatic activity with various actors, including the United States, have not yet led to a successful conclusion to date. At its October 24-25 2002 meeting, the European Council endorsed a document spelling out the EU interpretation of the modalities for the implementation of partici-pation by NATO non-EU European allies and mandated the high representative "to act accordingly for an agreement to be reached between the EU and NATO as soon as possible."[5]

EU-OSCE

As the largest contributor to the OSCE budget, the EU has exer-cised a major influence in the institutional developments and the operations of the OSCE where it enjoys the quasi-automatic support of the associated countries. Together with the U.S. and Russia, it has determined the course of the activities of the organization. The OSCE is a major framework for its foreign policy co-operation with Russia. The EU comprehensive approach to crisis management makes the OSCE an important partner for the EU, because of the overlap in areas of action in civilian crisis management.

The main areas of co-operation concern methods and instruments: compatibility of crisis management tools, interoperability of methods and standards, harmonization of recruitment and training standards, joint training activities, assistance in planning and establishment of OSCE missions. They also focus on functional and geographic priori-ties. Contacts and consultations between the relevant political bodies of the EU and OSCE are held at regular intervals. Working relations between the international bureaucracies and day-to-day co-operation in the field have been intensified.

EU-UN co-operation

The European Council has set specific priorities for areas of co-operation after extended consultations with the UN Secretariat. They cover mainly:

- Conflict prevention: ensuring mutually reinforcing activities, through regular consultations, fact-finding, exchange of infor-mation and assessments of potential or actual crises as well as co-operation in the field.

- Military and civilian crisis management: availability of EU military and civilian crisis management capacities for UN peace operations, compatibility of training standards, consultations on planning and implementation of crisis management, field co-ordination.

- Specific regional issues: Balkans, Middle East and Africa

Concrete modalities provide for regular consultations between the UN Secretary-General on the one hand and the EU Council and the EU High Representative and the Commissioner for External Relations on the other, the UN Secretary-General's relevant deputies and the Political and Security Committee of the EU. Working relations have been established between the international secretariats (as well as with the Commission on the EU side), in particular between the respective crisis management structures.

Looking towards the future

Any evaluation of the effectiveness of co-operation between institutions must be made in a dynamic perspective. It has to take into account the internal logic of their development, including changes in their membership as well and their capacity to adapt to a changing environment and to respond adequately to the needs of their individual members in the specific field of their competencies. The EU, NATO, the OSCE and the UN all continue to share an interest in European security. They have all been affected by the crises and the conflicts in Europe in the immediate post-Cold War period. The impact of these events and the policy responses of their individual member states as well as their degree of commitment to the goals of the organizations they belong to have done more to influence further institutional developments than any abstract grand design. On the other hand, the fact that the institutions adapted to changing circumstances and found a useful role in a new context constitutes a tribute to the flexibility and the soundness of their founding charters, as well as a reality check on the values shared by their individual members.

That does not mean that their co-operation cannot be improved and that they are perfectly complementary. It does not provide any guarantee that their agenda will never diverge and that improvement in co-operation is an unavoidable outcome. The specific culture of individual organizations and the national objectives member states pursue in each of them can sometimes account for contradictions or at least nuances in national positions according to the institutional framework within which they act. These national positions can also change over time. Developments in the perception of the threats and of vital interests have an impact on the evaluation made by an individual nation about the ability of a particular organization to take care of their evolving vision of the strategic environment. Overlap in membership is an important factor. So are differences in membership, which can become sometimes a more or less serious source of problems in co-operation between institutions, as is demonstrated in the case of the EU-NATO relationship.

The differences in nature between institutions, their overall missions and therefore, their institutional logic, have to be taken into account. In that sense, the EU has distinctive features of supranationality or pooling of sovereignty as well as globality of aims that are not shared by other institutions. This tends to put a premium on solidarity among EU member states. The fact that the EU nurtures the ambition to become an international actor as such, by gradually developing and enlarging the scope of its common foreign policy, will eventually not only affect the character of its relations with other international institutions, but also the missions, if not the nature of these institutions.

It has already happened as far as the OSCE is concerned. The EU's global approach to crisis management has resulted in the development of civil instruments and operational concepts in the field of police, rule of law, civil protection and institution and democracy building. In doing so, the EU clearly treads into areas of competence that had come to be seen as prerogatives of the OSCE. This trend is likely to accelerate functional and regional shifts in OSCE activities and priorities. The Vienna-based organization risks being pushed towards a status of subcontractor in the geographical area where EU membership is the ultimate stage of stabilization and reconstruction operations. Its leading role in conflict prevention and institution building will be left for the countries permanently outside the scope of EU integration. Its norm setting function in collective security for the Euro-Atlantic area could become its strongest asset.

NATO-EU and the transatlantic link

NATO and the EU have emerged as the two major players of European security. Their relation is central for the future of the European security architecture. As they have progressively ventured into each other's territory, the EU potentially assuming more of a military role and NATO a more political one, implementing the declared goal of strategic partnership is becoming increasingly important, if unhealthy competition or increased divergence are to be avoided. The unresolved issue of participation with Turkey illustrates the case that any EU-NATO arrangement, as good as it is on paper, will not be effective if mutual trust among all the member countries is not present. The real issue is not technical arrangements. In the case of Turkey it is about its place in Europe and its fear of being marginalized in NATO and in the EU. More fundamentally, the fate of EU-NATO relations hangs on the future course of transatlantic relations. All interested parties have to feel at ease with the way institutions fulfill their aspirations and goals, in this case more specifically how they satisfy or at least do not threaten their fundamental security and strategic interests.

A major development will have an impact on future trends: the dual enlargement of both institutions. Its effect should be to increase the convergence of their membership. This convergence could put pressure on some non-aligned member states of the EU to eventually choose to join NATO. The domestic debate in some of these countries shows that this is not just theoretical speculation. A mirror image debate is taking place in the European members of NATO who have so far eschewed EU membership.

It is obvious that overlap between NATO and EU membership could serve the cause of the strategic partnership. Several conditions remain to be satisfied for this outcome to become a reality.

The first one is of a political nature. Convergence in membership will help only if European members of EU and NATO do not approach their commitments in both institutions in conflicting terms.

A second one is the way each organization will cope with an enlarged membership as far as structures and procedures are concerned, especially in the field of decision-making. Political will is a pre-condition, but efficient institutions also matter a great deal. Good mechanisms for consensus building and for delegation in implementation of decisions call for the strengthening of the executive functions of the respective international structures and their heads. The NATO Secretary General and the EU Secretary General/High Representative will have to be given increased means of initiative and of action. That will raise tricky issues of political control by member states and of leadership within each institution. The EU faces a more complicated situation, with the pillar configuration, each with its own rules and procedures for decision-making and a different balance of competencies among the institutional actors. The leadership question is particularly sensitive, whereas the NATO situation is clearer in that respect. The rotating EU presidency has to be replaced by a more efficient system. The ongoing EU Convention on the future of the EU and the upcoming Intergovernmental Conference are supposed to find pertinent answers to these issues in terms of institutional reforms and political vision for the future of European integration.

Next, both EU and NATO will have to develop the appropriate tools to confront the new security challenges. Taking into account their different natures, the emphasis will have to be placed in complementarity and, where their competencies and fields of action overlap, compatibility and interoperability. Convergence of the tools and pursuit of a strategic partnership should be mutually reinforcing.

As far as the EU is concerned, access to NATO assets and capabilities is critical to fulfill the pledge not to engage in unnecessary duplications and rational use of resources as well as to compensate the shortfalls of European militaries in crucial strategic capabilities.

In order to be sustainable, such an arrangement has to be met by assurances from NATO that these assets and capabilities are adapted and remain relevant to the accomplishment of the military missions required in the context of rapidly evolving threats. This is particularly the case for the military command structures and the planning capabilities. Decisions at the Prague NATO summit will determine if the Allies accept the radical changes needed and the extent to which a real transformation will actually be implemented. Lack of progress in that respect, coupled with a continuing stalemate on the "Berlin plus" issue could result in increasing pressures towards "autonomous" European solutions and therefore in a process of duplication and de-coupling.

Given the apparent lack of willingness, at least in the short term, of the majority of European public opinions and governments to significantly increase resources for defense and even to quickly adopt concrete measures for a better use of existing ones, a widening resources and capability gap between the U.S. and its allies constitutes the biggest risk to bring about the sort of de-coupling that would harm the prospects of a mutually beneficial EU-NATO co-operation. Improving capabilities is on the agenda of both organizations. The main vehicles are the "new" DCI and the European Capability Action Plan. Within the scope of these processes, the Europeans will have to produce a significant effort in order to improve their military capabilities and agree to a better balance in sharing the burden of security in Europe and beyond.

The chances for such an improvement actually happening are a question of political will. Europeans have to face the hard choices between competing priorities. Strong political leadership has been elusive in articulating the price to pay for security and the preservation of a model of society. Much more progress is needed towards a common European assessment of present and future threats and convergent visions of the policy instruments to be used in dealing with them.

In that sense, two kinds of gaps have to be filled: the first is a transatlantic one; the other is a gap among Europeans themselves. In the latter case, narrowing down the differences between European traditions in foreign policy goals and instruments, in particular intervention in crises, including the use of force, is the main challenge for achieving an effective and credible European common foreign and security policy. Reaching that goal and improving the tools of CFSP, which is indispensable to ESDP, would make the European point of view more convincing in the dialogue with the U.S. on security and defense issues. The alternative would push the ESDP towards irrelevance.

EU-NATO and the transatlantic relation in the post September 11th world.

Strengthening ESDP and eventually enlarging its scope (to confront new threats such as terrorism and WMD), implementing a more ambitious and more effective common European foreign policy in the context of an enlarged EU, combined with convergence if not overlap in membership between NATO and EU, will gradually shift the focus on EU-U.S. relations rather than on EU-NATO relations. NATO could and should remain the instrument of choice for transatlantic political and military co-operation, for confronting common security challenges wherever they arise, while remaining a strong defensive alliance. But the new security challenges demand more than a military response. If the U.S. shows a readiness to accept the value of "soft power" and the EU accepts the necessity to use military force more decisively when needed, a more global partnership could also emerge, in which the partners choose the pertinent institutional framework as a function of the goals to pursue.

There lie the conditions for a rededication of the transatlantic partnership. At stake is finding the kind of international order—and the instruments necessary to bring it about—on which both partners are able to agree. The question is therefore whether the Atlantic will remain a bridge or become a growing divide.

In the past, the U.S. has always set the agenda and the pace of change. There is little prospect for this pattern to be different in the immediate future. The United States was the main architect of the UN system and of the international financial institutions to serve as tools to shape the world according to its vision after WWII. It was the cornerstone for the strength and the cohesion of the Atlantic alliance, in the defense of Western democracies that led to the defeat of the Soviet bloc in the Cold War. The U.S. again led the Alliance to its transformation in the aftermath of the fall of the Berlin Wall, allowing it to play a central role in the stabilization of the Balkans and the Euro-Atlantic area.

All these developments took place with European support and substantial European contributions. Multilateralism and institutionalized cooperation were basic tenets of the transatlantic partnership.

Europeans have contributed substantially to the strength of this strategic partnership. But they have always tended to act primarily in a reactive mode. When they have built common policies and gained a measure of strategic autonomy, it was generally to fill the void left by the U.S., with more or less American support or tolerance. The U.S. has always been ambivalent about such developments. Calls for more equitable security burden sharing have regularly been balanced by efforts to keep European ambitions in check.

The new parameters of the security environment have been exposed for some time. Evidence of their reality have emerged in the course of the Balkans conflicts. But September 11th has opened the eyes of the world on their destructive potential and on the global character of security challenges. As a result, the traditional geographic approach to defense has become obsolete. Time has replaced territory as the focus for strategic advantage. In order to deal with the new threats, the ability to quickly identify, analyze and react to them, either through prevention or through suppression, is of the essence.

The fact that the U.S. was the target of the attacks has accelerated there the ongoing evolution of the strategic doctrine and the revolution in military affairs designed to deliver the capabilities to deal with the new threats. Europe has clearly been slow to emulate.

The new U.S. National Security Strategy has set the stage for a comprehensive vision on how America sees its role and responsibilities, now that it "possesses unprecedented- and unequalled- strength and influence in the world."[6] In practice, the Wilsonian vision outlined in this document is seen and experienced by many as a choice to follow a unilateralist course of action in dealing with international affairs. Concerns are expressed that the United States is using its self defined-status as a "benign hegemon" as a justification to define the rules of the game alone and to be the only judge of their respect by others. The professed intentions not to allow the emergence of any strategic rival or peer, the American selective disengagement from international regimes and preference for flexible coalitions according to circumstances are presented as evidence. The legitimization of pre-emption and of regime changes creates fears of anarchy in the system of international relations.

As far as European security is concerned, it raises questions among allies about the degree of commitment the U.S. keeps in NATO as an alliance. They fear an evolution of NATO towards a military toolbox for building coalitions of the willing at the service of U.S. strategic interests or towards a loose collective security, essentially political forum. If this commitment fades away, it could increase the risk of a decline of the strong institutional framework that has characterized European security for the last half century and spell a return to the re-nationalization of defense policies.

This outcome is not unavoidable. The fact that the U.S. administration has been convinced to go the UN route in dealing with the Iraq WMD issue is a sign that they can be influenced by allies and friends and see the value of legitimacy conferred by acting in a multilateral framework.

Once again the U.S. has set the agenda. Once again this is a challenge for the Europeans to take up. There is still a lot more common ground and interdependence than differences across the Atlantic in areas such as trade, investment and fundamental societal values for preserving and nurturing this essential partnership. A new transatlantic deal will have to be struck. As far as the strategic dimension is concerned, it must rest on two basic conditions: a common assessment of the threats and an agreement on the ways to deal with them. The EU would have to shed the structural weaknesses of its strategic culture and its political reluctance to acquire and to use the instruments of power when needed. The U.S. will have to recognize the value of "soft power" and the considerable potential of the model of integration that the EU provides for other regions of the world and which it continues to promote as an essential component of its common foreign policy.

Under such a deal, the coalition around shared values will continue to define the mission. It is a formula that has been successfully tested for more than half a century. It still enjoys the support of the majority of public opinion on both sides of the Atlantic, as recent polls have shown. It offers a much better guarantee for a stable international order than the opposite proposition.

Notes:

1. Felipe Fernandez Armesto, Civilizations, Macmillan, 2000.

2. For NATO, see the Washington Treaty; for the EU, see the Treaty of the European Union; for the OSCE, the Helsinki Final Act, the Charter of Paris and the Istanbul Charter of European Security. All documents available on the websites of the respective organisations.

3. Washington Summit communiqué; see http://www.nato.int/docu/pr/1999.

4. Nice European Council, 7, 8 and 9 December 2000; annex vi to the Presidency conclusions, Presidency report on the European Security and Defense Policy, page 37; see www.europa.eu.int.

5. Presidency conclusions, European Council, October 24-25, 2002; SN 300/02; see www.europa.eu.int.

6. The National Security Strategy of the United States of America, September 2002, the White House.

Counting Capabilities: What For?

Antonio Missiroli

Despite the official rhetoric, the Capabilities Improvement Conference held in Brussels in November 2001—meant to check on the implementation of the Helsinki Headline Goal[1]—was not a particularly satisfactory exercise. Of course, the objective has been essentially met and it looks likely that the European Rapid Reaction Force will be declared "fully operational," as planned, in 2003. Whilst the absolute numbers pledged by the member states look impressive (100,000 men and women, 400 aircraft and 100 naval elements), however, most of those forces are "double-hatted" (i.e. they are also answerable to NATO, in principle, and possibly already engaged in current operations), no additional capabilities have been created, and overlaps of irrelevant ones coexist with persisting shortages in key areas. The main shortfalls are well known: strategic lift and tactical transport, surveillance, command-control-communications and intelligence (C3-I) and sophisticated combat capabilities. The European Capabilities Action Plan (ECAP) released at the Conference, however, is not a detailed plan for time-bound actions but rather a set of guiding principles for EU military cooperation. They include increased effectiveness of the capability effort, a bottom-up approach to defense cooperation with commitments on a voluntary basis, and coordination between member states and with NATO in the Headline Task Force-plus framework, essential to target specific shortcomings. Yet the only "action" foreseen is further monitoring, albeit coupled with peer pressure. This is the limit of the whole exercise: meeting the goals and filling the gaps is entirely left to the goodwill of the member states, without appropriate incentives and rewards for doing so. And this is a pity, given the ample opportunities that exist for pooling, rationalisation and collaboration among Europeans—both bi- and multi-laterally—*and* at the EU level.

On the rationale for increasing defense spending in order to tackle both the transatlantic "capabilities gap"[2] and the specifically European capabilities problem, however, opinions and visions still differ—and sometimes diverge—inside the EU. A discussion paper circulated late last year by the King's College Center for Defense Studies, based on a joint research project with five other European institutes, showed for instance that the scope of the "Petersberg tasks" is not interpreted in the same way inside the EU. There certainly is a broad consensus among officials over their "low-end," for which most of the necessary resources—including those related to non-military crisis management—are already available both across the Union (through member states) and in Brussels (through the Commission's Rapid Reaction Mechanism, ECHO, Europ-Aid, plus the Council Secretariat). "High end" missions, instead, are much more controversial and their understanding seems differently nuanced even among the six main military players in the EU. For Sweden and Germany, for instance, the upper limit of an Art. 17 Treaty on European Union (TEU) operation coincides—by analogy, so to speak—with IFOR/SFOR or KFOR ("peacekeeping" proper). For France and Italy, the upper limit would be the 1991 Desert Storm campaign, considered to be "restoring order." Italy, however, would undertake that type of operation only in cooperation with NATO. For the UK and the Netherlands, tolerance extends to the 1999 Allied Force deemed to be "crisis management" proper. Differences do not necessarily lie in the amount of military forces involved on the ground—although air power varies significantly—but rather in the description and the mandate of the envisaged mission.[3] Such nuances would probably cover an even wider spectrum if all fifteen member states (let alone the candidates for accession) were brought into the picture. And, needless to say, the scarcity of adequate European assets for "high end" operations makes military cooperation with NATO a crucial issue. The deal with Turkey on "Berlin-plus," if and when finalised, would also facilitate the non-duplication of planning structures.[4] That would be very helpful both functionally and politically for ESDP, but per se would not solve the shortfalls problem.

Nor does DCI, actually. First of all, NATO's record in meeting pre-set capability goals—insofar as the European allies are concerned—has traditionally been modest, to say the least. Many reasons contributed to that: Europeans relied on the U.S. for the substance of collective defense, the division of labour inside the Alliance left command & control and key capabilities mainly to the U.S. (while the Europeans provided manpower and land-based assets that are of little use now), and even the financial deals were such that European money was channelled elsewhere and, in any case, not invested in a forward-looking manner. Since the end of the Cold War, only Britain and (to a much lesser extent) France have managed to preserve or develop their power projection capabilities, and that well outside of NATO planning. They have done so for reasons related to their national interests and through reforms of the military that were not related to NATO goals. The other European allies have first reaped their peace dividends, then long hesitated before undertaking structural reforms. When they have eventually moved in that direction—the Benelux countries first, followed by France, Italy and, albeit less consistently, Germany[5]—the driving force has been less compliance with NATO guidelines than a mix of financial constraints, functional demands, and European ambitions. For them, in fact, the ultimate wake-up call was Operation Allied Force, coming as it did at the end of a very frustrating decade in the Balkans. However, the list of shortfalls enshrined in the DCI, as released in the wake of the operation, was way too ambitious and out of step with the realities of Europe's financial leeway and political will. As a result, it has been largely ignored by most European allies: they have started addressing the decline in defense spending only recently and with a view to tackling only those shortfalls (strategic lift and satellite imagery) that may serve also for ESDP, i.e. below the foreseeable "high end" threshold and well below high-tech combat capabilities. For the Americans, in turn, the DCI seems to have represented more a useful tool for Europe-bashing than a carefully conceived blueprint for improving overall NATO assets (and the European share thereof). This may help understand why the Alliance plans to review its DCI goals and to reduce them from 50-odd to less then 10, but with a more realistic and stringent timetable.

On top of that, the marginal increases in defense expenditure recently adopted by some EU members—yet again, however, Britain and more recently France represent the most conspicuous cases in point—are still too modest to reverse the trend, while the effects of domestic military reforms will be felt only later on. The A 400 M project shenanigans provide further evidence of the persisting problems: it is telling that last summer's floods in Central Europe have put its financing schemes into question. In addition, the dead end in which the "Berlin-plus" framework seems to remain, coupled with the doubts over the future of NATO that mar transatlantic relations since October 2001, impact negatively upon what has long been considered the most likely context for an improvement of European capabilities, namely that of peace support/Art. 17 TEU operations on the continent under a NATO flag but with predominant European forces on the ground.[6] The European role, in other words, was defined by the self-imposed limits of U.S. power: it seemed meagre, at first glance, but it was substantial and had implications for the way in which European think about their defense/military priorities. Now that the U.S. strategic interest in being a European power seems to be waning, the rationale for developing, at best, complementary rather than parallel force structures to the American ones might lose its stringency. Even if the emphasis shifts on "*constructive* duplication,"[7] however, the problem of defense spending remains—and worsens.

The problem is all the more difficult to address because of:

- The lack of tangible strategic threats to the EU "homeland." Not even September 11th and its aftermath have triggered a U-turn in defense spending across the Union, and what has been done by the Union in the fight against terrorism has been either bilateral and outside the NATO framework (military support), or EU-internal and primarily civilian;

- What one may call *inevitable* duplications: member states' forces cannot be considered (nor counted or treated) as a single unit, unlike the American ones. There certainly are *unnecessary* duplications, and we should aim at some necessary duplications of capabilities vis-à-vis the U.S. (especially as far as strategic assets are concerned). Yet it is still unthinkable for EU members (including smaller ones) to give up e.g. on entire armed services and resources that are considered part of the constitutional tasks of any state;

- The sociological constraints that derive in part from European demography (aging societies) and in part from established welfare entitlements.[8] Overhauling public expenditure and diverting resources from pensions (or agriculture!) to defense is a daunting task for political leaders: it takes time and it does not bring electoral dividends. Citizens and voters tend to give priority to internal protection over external projection—hence an in-built rigidity that cannot be ignored or just blamed;

- Last but not least, the financial and budgetary constraints imposed by the stability and growth pact for the euro, now also combined with the apparent slowdown of Western economies in the wake of September 11. For the EU members, a dramatic increase in defense (and "homeland" security) expenditure like the one adopted by the Bush administration after the terrorist attacks is simply unimaginable.

How to deal, then, with all these constraints?

The issue of how to increase defense spending for European crisis management was first addressed publicly in the wake of St. Malo and the 1999 Cologne European Council. At that time, the debate revolved around the applicability of the political and functional logic of European Monetary Union (EMU) to the fledgling ESDP, thus replicating what was widely seen as a success story. In fact, possible "convergence criteria" were canvassed, desirable minimal targets for current national defense expenditure (2 to 2.5 % of GDP) or for new investments (0.7 %) were mentioned. Such a *"demand-led"* approach aimed at setting quantitative indicators that were partially arbitrary (not unlike the EMU criteria, for that matter) and questionable (simply bloating the budgets of ministries of defense is not that difficult, in principle, but it does not necessarily generate the required capabilities) while imposing no real constraints: unlike EMU, no penalties were envisaged for non-compliance. Besides, the underlying paradox of the whole discussion was that the "convergence criteria" for the euro had been set by finance ministers to curb public expenditure across the board, whereas those for ESDP were being put forward by foreign and/or defense ministers to "free" public expenditure in one sector only—with all the risks of a chain reaction on the part of other ministries, that would have ended up jeopardising EMU.[9]

This prospect, British idiosyncrasy for EMU terminology, and the impact of the Kosovo war contributed to channelling the debate towards a *"supply-led"* approach, based on voluntary contributions, pledges, peer review and best practice. Such was the logic behind the Headline Goal and its subsequent implementation and follow-up. Much as the exercise has contributed to speeding domestic reforms of the military (especially in Italy and Germany), it has delivered limited results in both budgetary and functional/operational terms. Rises in national defense budgets have been minimal across the Union, and even the pooling of forces has been driven mainly—if not exclusively—by a political and/or symbolic rationale. In fact, only few of the European multi-national forces created over the past ten years or so are fully certified by NATO and deployable as such for significant operations.

Is it possible to combine somewhat the two approaches described above and generate some momentum and additional incentives for a) getting higher value for money (spending *better*), and b) freeing more resources for "defense" (spending *more*)? Some serious pooling of defense expenditure seems the only realistic and viable way of meeting such goals:

- Indirectly and in the longer term, through some *role specialisation* for both capabilities/forces and assets/materiel. This could imply the allocation of specific functional roles to certain member states, in particular smaller ones: it may not do away entirely with "unnecessary" duplications, but it may improve effectiveness and foster consolidation across the EU board. Role specialisation, however, presupposes, entails and eventually requires a higher level of political integration and a substantial lack of immediate territorial threats: either condition (or both) may not be acceptable or applicable to *all* present and future member states;

- In the medium term, through a common (not necessarily a single!) *procurement policy* and a less protected *market for defense* industry. Three main moves could be tentatively made in this domain (sort of pillar "one-and-a-half"): first, the ever more necessary loosening of Art. 296 of the Treaty Establishing the European Community (TEC, as amended by the 1997 Treaty of Amsterdam), that basically exempts trade in defense goods from the rules of the internal EU market; second, some refurbishment of the TEU provisions on "enhanced cooperation" in order to permit limited and pre-determined forms thereof for specific industrial projects (space, surveillance, strategic lift); third, agreeing on specific modalities (including perhaps exceptions to the stability pact) that could facilitate common R & D expenditure;

- In the short term, through the creation of some *EU-funded supranational force elements*. An interesting model in this same field is the one adopted by NATO for its AWACS aircraft. Its method of sharing costs and risks and benefits while training multinationally-manned crews could well apply to many existing but still sputtering common European projects (from A 400 M to aircraft-carriers). A possible funding model, instead, is the one offered within the EU by the European Development Fund (EDF). The EDF was created in the early 1990s separately from Community aid. It is not based on a GDP key but on a voluntary and ever modifiable formula. It is not an invoice in the EU budget (therefore not under any control of the European Parliament or the Commission); and it is not just a sum of national contributions. By the same token, a European Defense (or Capabilities) Fund could be set up and could fill the existing gap between the general willingness to cooperate and the lack of available and reliable on-call resources. Participating EU countries should identify a small number of uncontroversial near-term projects where a useful military capability could be provided on a pooled basis but well beyond the old logic of "*juste retour*" that keeps haunting the European defense industry;

- Finally, some common principles could be agreed to *measure* national contributions to ESDP: money, assets, manpower, know-how, and/or combinations thereof. This is also meant to prevent the emergence of a "burden-sharing" debate inside the EU and among Europeans at large (between "haves" and "have-nots," security providers and free-riders) as well as to add legitimacy and transparency to the whole process.

All these ideas, however, bet on ESDP as the main (if not sole) driver of a significant increase in European defense spending and resulting capabilities: an increase that, anyway, would stop short of the hi-tech capabilities that now seem the cornerstone of the U.S. strategic doctrine and, in spite of the growing convergence of approach that has emerged lately between the ECAP and the DCI, would hardly fill the ever growing "capabilities gap."

This said, there are some political considerations to be made here. On the one hand, it is simply not correct to say that Europeans do not spend enough for security or crisis management. Not only do European forces and officials (let alone funds) largely outnumber American ones on the ground in the Balkans. Even in Afghanistan the main burden of nation-building and reconstruction rests on European shoulders. Paradoxically, also the future of NATO and its continued relevance—contrary to previous assumptions—may now end up depending, at least in part, on whether ESDP succeeds or not: suffice it to look at the discussions over Operation Amber Fox in Macedonia and its possible takeover by the Union in conjunction with the Alliance.

Conversely, the fight against terrorism seems to have taken completely different avenues, basically sidelining NATO and hardly affecting the original scope of ESDP. Even when the Union talks of its own "civil defense," the relevant measures are hardly related to Alliance initiatives or plans (and even less so to "Homeland Defense" in the U.S.).[10] It remains to be seen whether the proposal, recently made by the U.S. Secretary of Defense, to build a "high end" NATO response force to fight terrorism worldwide will find the necessary consensus to take off. If so, it could give the Alliance a brand new role and mission—global and primarily "out-of-area"—that would, in turn, make it ever more complicated fully to preserve the old (Article 5) and especially the recent (non-Article 5) ones.

This is only to say that if the most urgent and appropriate objective of ESDP is gradually to take over control and administration of the Balkans, preserve law and order in the region, and provide a political framework for peace-building and future integration, the whole discussion over the "capabilities gap" is, to a certain extent, superfluous and even misleading. If ESDP, in other words, is to be primarily an "in-area" regional stabilisation policy, the European Union already has the necessary resources and capabilities: the Headline Goal was set having in mind IFOR/SFOR, not Allied Force (and even less Enduring Freedom). The geographical scope for EU-led missions is broadly defined as "in and around Europe,"[11] and its basic modality a smooth and gradual devolution of NATO and/or U.S.-led tasks—which is exactly what is happening in the Balkans, starting with the police operation in Bosnia. After all, there is no need any more for full-spectrum or "escalation dominance" vis-à-vis a nasty local actor; no need any more for strategic lift (after the initial problems, the personnel are now on the ground); no need any more for highly sophisticated satellite surveillance; even less for suppression of air defenses or precision-guided weapons. The Balkans are increasingly turning into a

European "protectorate": that now requires long-term political and financial commitment, not "high-end" combat capabilities. Operations there are likely to be "mixed" ones, with a military component coupled with police and judicial presence, plus technical and economic assistance and the degree of political "conditionality" that the EU has already applied to the current candidates. This is precisely what the Union is already good at, although it may end up absorbing most of its limited resources and straining its internal financial solidarity.

If, instead, ESDP is to be much more ambitious and aim at building a strategic global partnership with the U.S. (well beyond the traditional NATO area and mandate)—the "axis of good," so to speak—then the abovementioned shortfalls in European capabilities have to be addressed accordingly and swiftly. In order to do so, however, the incentives cannot come only from inside the European Union (or NATO as such). It looks difficult, in fact, to convince public opinion across Europe to invest dramatically on defense and combat capabilities if U.S. doctrine and rhetoric stress the primacy of missions over coalitions, of unilateral over multilateral action, of U.S. industrial and technological monopoly over diversification and sharing. In other words, while the Europeans have to decide whether they still want to fight alongside the Americans (and, if so, prepare and take the appropriate measures), the Americans, too, have to make up their mind about the extent to which they still want like-minded partners and allies on board and take consequent and coherent steps—inside and outside NATO.

Notes:

1. The Headline Goal was set by the Helsinki European Council in December 1999. It aimed at establishing by 2003 a Rapid Reaction Force the size of an army corps (50/60, 000 men), supported by the appropriate air and naval elements, and deployable within 60 days for at least one year. Cf. M. Rutten (comp.), *From St. Malo to Nice—European Defense: Core Documents*, Chaillot Paper n.47, WEU ISS, Paris, May 2001, pp.82 ss. (www.iss-eu.org).

2. See D.Jost, *The NATO Capabilities Gap and the European Union*, "Survival," XLII, n.4, Winter 2000-2001, pp.97-128.

3. Centre for Defense Studies, *Achieving the Helsinki Headline Goals*, Discussion Paper, November 2001, King's College, London.

4. On the whole issue cf. A.Missiroli, *EU-NATO Cooperation in Crisis Management: No Turkish Delight for ESDP*, "Security Dialogue," vol. 33, no.1, March 2002, pp.9-26.

5. Since 1992 Belgium, the Netherlands, France, Luxembourg, Spain, Italy and Portugal have moved to professional armies (Ireland and the UK did so long ago), while almost all the others have preserved conscription coupled with more specialized units.

6. Actually, such has become increasingly the case in the Balkans: as of March 2002, SFOR encompassed 13,300 personnel from the EU-15 and 3,850 from the U.S. (out of a total of almost 20,000), KFOR approx. 26,500 from the EU-15 and 5,300 from the U.S. (out of approx. 40,000). In EU lingo, such operations are called "Petersberg tasks" (from the WEU Declaration of June 1992) and incorporated since 1999 in Art. 17 of the Treaty on European Union.

7. See e.g. K.Schake, *Constructive Duplication: Reducing EU reliance on U.S. Military Assets*, CER Working Paper, London, January 2002 (www.cer.org.uk).

8. Cf. i.a. C.Lachaux, *Alliance Atlantique et Europe de la défense: les faits sont têtus*, "Défense Nationale," LV, n.8/9, aout-septembre 1999, pp.80-86.

9. Cf. A.Missiroli, *European Security and Defense: The Case for Setting 'Convergence Criteria,'* "European Foreign Affairs Review," IV, n.4, Winter 1999, pp.485-500.

10. See S.Duke, *CESDP and the EU Response to 11 September: Identifying the Weakest Link*, "European Foreign Affairs Review," VII, n.2, Summer 2002, pp.153-169.

11. More technically, the maximum radius is set—as a planning assumption—at 4,000 Km from Brussels (or average sailing distance from the member States), which soars to 10,000 Km for purely humanitarian tasks.

Projecting European Power:
A European View

Ralph Thiele

"The European Union has long had access to a wide range of tools with which to help provide security and engage with the rest of the world. This has not so far included military capabilities. But this is now changing. The Union's new security and defense policy will fill a gap in the instruments available to us. It will include both military and civilian capabilities, and is designed to give us the option, should we choose to do so, of intervening in crisis management operations. It is not about the projection of power. Europe's imperial days have long since past into history. But it is about security—our security, and others' security."[1]
Javier Solana—High Representative for the Common Foreign and Security Policy

21st century security

Today, no European state is any longer capable of guaranteeing its security on a purely national basis. It is not even possible to pursue security policy in a comprehensive sense at European Union borders. Instead, the global dimensions have to be considered. Globalization and migration movements, the vulnerability of modern industrial societies as well as global and asymmetrical governmental and non-governmental protagonists call for a new understanding of national security which concentrates on the multinational protection of populations and the critical infrastructure.[2]

With regard to the increasing vulnerability of the intricate post-industrial societies, in which the survival of individuals depends not only on the availability of food, water and energy, but also on a multitude of information services—that can easily be threatened by governmental protagonists or new, "non-governmental" actors using asymmetric force—, the long-term economic, political, financial and socio-cultural base of the modern state needs effective protection. Intervention is possible from nearly any point on earth so that the risks cannot be handled with purely defensive instruments. At the same time, it is becoming increasingly difficult to determine the quality of the threshold of a criminal action within a state as an act of war.

Today's world of states—roughly two hundred entities—seems to be becoming a fiction in many places around the globe. Quite a number of states seem to be disintegrating, resulting in both domestic and interstate irregularities, which jeopardize the international order. According to analyses of the World Bank,[3] the world's non-governmental actors are using organized force—including war—as a means of enforcing their economic interests and those of their clients. The object is in most cases to exploit resources in the territories under their control, exploit the population or siphon off international assistance, often in connection with forms of internationally organized crime. These activities reach far into the national economies of the OECD world. They encourage corruption and organized crime and undermine national and international economies.

In such an environment, warfare is no longer purely directed against the military potential of adversarial states. It is rather directed at infiltrating all areas of their societies and to threaten their existences. The comparatively easy access to weapons of mass destruction, in particular relatively low-cost biological agents, is of key concern. Both governmental and non-governmental actors prefer to use force in a way that can be characterized as "unconventional" or also as "small wars." War waged according to conventions is an interstate phenomenon. The "small war" is the archetype of war, in which the protagonists acknowledge no rules and permanently try to violate what conventions do exist. The protagonists of the "small war" observe neither international standards nor arms control agreements. They make use of territories where they do not have to fear any sanctions because there is no functioning state to assume charge of such sanctions or because the state in question is too weak to impose such sanctions. This type of war does not provide for any warning time. It challenges not only the external security of the nation states and international community, but also their internal safety.

Like external security, which nation states have been unable to guarantee on their own for some time, in the future, internal safety also will have to be maintained increasingly by states engaging in joint action and coordinating measures and drawing on the help of international organizations. This entails new and unavoidable aspects of future security policy. Besides the preservation of the present world order and the prevention of interstate wars, which jeopardize international security, the limitation and containment of "small wars" will gain considerable importance in the future. This calls for a security policy which recognizes that it has to be suitable for dealing both with governmental actors which function more or less well, and those non-governmental protagonists that employ organized force; and, therefore, which are able to endanger not only international security, but also the external security and internal safety of individual states.

To integrate these non-governmental actors into a world order which reduces force and strengthens security will probably become one of the primary missions of the international community for the coming decades. Security policy needs to be adapted to these developments. Societies have to realize that national and regional security structures will not be sufficient to protect their security against global challenges—neither internally nor externally. Security policy has to be understood as a global creative task of the international community. That will only work if the states make an integrated, common and multinational effort.

Consequently, the essential elements of a 21st century security policy will be:

- further development of collective security,

- reinforcement of the states' exclusive right to use force,

- strengthening of the civilizational forces (good governance) and

- containment of the phenomenon of "small wars" (i.e. the development of concepts for small-scale warfare and intervention, arms control in the age of small-scale warfare, small-scale warfare and economy as well as small-scale warfare and international law).

Although today the United States is the only global power left, this will not remain the case forever as Paul Kennedy has pointed out in his remarkable analytical study, *The Rise and Fall of the Great Powers*.[4] The challenge is to establish a dynamic stable international order within the framework of a cooperative multipolarity—with the U.S., the European Union, Russia, China and India as key actors—based on the steadily increasing mutual dependence of the national economic systems within the scope of globalization. It must ensure the advancement of civilization, which allows the satisfaction of the economic, social and cultural needs of an ever-increasing number of people. The goal of the international order must be to prevent governmental and non-governmental protagonists from trying to influence this process by war. For this purpose, a comprehensive set of foreign and security policy instruments and capabilities must be developed which also includes military assets.

Capable of global action

To do this, however, it is not enough for only the U.S. to shoulder global responsibility and be willing to take on burdens to support the development of other regions; rich Europe must also exercise its global responsibility by "burden-sharing." Only then can states such as Russia, China and India be called upon to make the same efforts. To this end, Europe holds the key to a cooperative world order in its own hands. Should the U.S.—overstrained by having to play a global hegemonic role—withdraw, global and regional hegemony conflicts would follow. Such a development would force all the nation states to spend enormous sums on risk prevention of the resulting classical security dilemma[5] and there would hardly be any resources left for managing the risks which are threatening mankind as a whole and its civilizational advancement. Under these circumstances, the European nation states can no longer play independent, individual roles in world politics as the weight of each on its own is insufficient. Through the process of European integration, they have to develop into a power capable of global action.

With the completion of the Single Market and the common currency, the very logic of European integration makes it particularly urgent to satisfy the demand for an effective foreign and security policy, including the ability to use force when necessary. The crises in the Balkans have revealed the serious limitations the European Union faces as it tries to deal with these new circumstances. Another factor is that the new strategic priorities of the United States—towards the Pacific and towards counterterrorism—underline the fact that they may not be willing to intervene in every crisis in and around Europe.

While today's security problems are very different from those in the Cold War period, many are a product of that very period. We are still dealing with these consequences in regions such as the Balkans and the Middle East. The EU is also committed to creating lasting peace and stability in the Balkans and has expressed its strategic interest in the stability of the Mediterranean region and the Caucasus. As Javier Solana states: "[P]eace and stability in the Middle East are among our fundamental interests, both for reasons of geographical proximity and because of the risks we might run were there to be prolonged instability in the region."[6]

Instability, conflict and deprivation lead people to flee their own countries. Integrating refugees and accepting economic migrants are difficult issues and pose huge challenges for Europe. These problems are on our doorstep. The population projections for Europe on the one hand and North Africa on the other speak for themselves. But such problems are not limited to Europe and its neighbors. Instability anywhere can undermine Europe's interests. Russia's choices are of particular importance for Europe. In that context and in view of a historic enlargement, Europe has no option but to become more engaged in the international arena.

A particular legacy of the Cold War is the continuing existence of large numbers of weapons of mass destruction. The collapse of the Soviet Union has encouraged the spread of nuclear technology. The likelihood of weapons of mass destruction falling into the hands of criminals and terrorists is a real threat today. Other, new forms of terrorist activity are beginning to emerge in the form of biotech weapons and large-scale computer sabotage. Europe's security, prosperity and well-being depend on how effectively these challenges are met.

The nature of the likely crises and their protagonists along an arc of potential crises from the Caucasus to the Maghreb will make it particularly appropriate for the European Union to organize Western responses. Crises in this area notably reflect the problems posed by fragile states, demographic change, economic weakness and poor governance. Managing them requires a classical European soft security approach rather than the classical U.S. hard line. The challenge is "nation-building" and the European Union's security model is likely to be more acceptable in the regions concerned—and very likely even more effective in the long term. Compared to the U.S., Europe is particularly effective in stability operations. Consequently, much of the emphasis will be on peacekeeping and conventional peacemaking, an area in which European forces excel, while the U.S. tends to avoid such commitments. Robust military operations in that environment will likely require only small numbers of highly-trained special forces, and Europe already has some of these.

Developing the European Union into a pole in a multipolar world order, able to act globally and which helps to develop human civilization, helps meet the challenges of the future. Consequently, a European security policy should aim to establish a transatlantic-Asiatic security zone. It should support common efforts undertaken by the international community in zones that jeopardize international security. It should also contribute to international security, concerted development policy, as well as to the development of international and regional structures for the management of transnational problems. Altogether, this analysis calls for the strengthening of Europe's capacity to influence developments in the world and to help shape that world according to its values and interests. The aim is to create an efficient crisis management capability, including the use of military force, utilizing all the instruments available to the Union and its member states and wielding them in support of Common Foreign and Security Policy objectives.

The European Union has a wide range of non-military capabilities at its disposal to influence developments all over the globe. As a global economic player, these capabilities include cooperation agreements, trade policy instruments, development assistance and various other forms of economic and social policy. Therefore, the projection of European power cannot be confined to the classical meaning of employing military force to defend narrow, national interests. On the contrary, it needs to be a much broader concept based on fundamental, collective interests. Yet, the possibility and the capability to project military forces need to be viable elements within the set of available military options.

In view of this, Europe's Common Foreign and Security Policy needs to be developed into a comprehensive strategy. It particularly needs to take account of crisis prevention and the post-crisis period rather than focusing only on ending a conflict. Options for EU involvement are worldwide. While the main area of concern needs to be Europe itself and its periphery, the future spectrum of options and reservoir of capabilities must also allow the EU to contribute to peace and stability anywhere in the world.

Prevention needed

Currently, the European Union's planning process still focuses on three generic scenarios:

- assistance to civilians,
- conflict prevention/preventive deployment and
- separation of parties by force.

These scenarios are principally still based on earlier planning activities of the Western European Union (WEU). The scenarios are neither limiting nor binding, just food for thought. But, that is all Europe has to offer in conceptual planning at this stage. Consequently, European defense efforts tend to rest on these considerations—focussing predominantly on the lower-tech, lower-intensity end of the conflict spectrum. Peacekeeping mechanisms are valuable assets, but the European Headline Goals (EHG) and the Petersberg tasks have to be developed further.

Within the new security environment, prevention is of particular importance in every respect, because of the potential damage that may be caused in future conflicts and the possible consequences for people and economic and social development. The time dimension—since there will be no sufficient warning time and no long-term trends—will only allow the authorities in a few cases to wait and see what damage is caused before reacting to a threat. In those cases with far-reaching consequences—e.g. in which there is a threat to the very survival of nations and to their economic and social development—priority must be given to preventive action. Moreover, a policy aimed at prevention will encourage economic development and reduce the overall costs. Prevention is a key challenge for human civilization in modern times.

Consequently, prevention needs to be given priority in the concert of the security policy instruments. The advancement of the international order towards a world in which there is less force as well as the encouragement of civilizational development and the containment of the phenomena of the small war are the fundamentals of such a prevention policy and instrumental in reducing the causes of violence and in establishing non-violent mechanisms for conflict management.

Preventing war and consolidating peace will be the most important tasks of the armed forces of Europe and their transatlantic partners in the decades to come. Consequently the European Security and Defense Policy has to

- prevent or put an end to interstate wars in Europe and neighboring areas;

- limit or control "small wars" in these areas;

- contribute to the global control of weapons of mass destruction;

- contribute globally to the capabilities of the U.S. and other states, which are interested in a common world order in the above-mentioned sense of prevention and limitation of militarily organized force.

The challenge

To achieve and secure a non-violent international order, the two most important strategic objectives of future security policy will be the establishment of a cooperative multipolar world order and the prevention and containment of interstate and "small wars." Consequently, the development of the military instruments of the international community will head in the direction of enabling successful intervention. This approach requires military capabilities which support deterrence by denial—i.e. the real capacity to deprive one or several states or non-governmental actors of the capability to wage war.

What are needed to influence developments on the ground and enforce the political purpose are defensive *and* offensive military capabilities which allow both military control of and influence over the protagonists. Of course, the capabilities associated with waging war are not only of a purely material nature. The legitimate right to wage war, for example, is of particular importance. In the recent past, there has been hardly any military conflict in which the protagonists did not employ a public relations company to justify their legitimate right to wage war or to question that of the enemy. The result of wars is to a considerable degree determined by this debate.

Considering all the experience available, there will be two essential tasks for the armed forces in the future: One is to win the conflict militarily in a rapid and decisive manner—predominantly from a distance. The other is to consolidate the military success on the ground. Both tasks support the political purpose. There is no imperative sequence for them, so the focus of action between decision and consolidation can shift in the course of an operation and is determined largely by the protagonists.

The military superiority of the intervention forces will probably prevent a conflict from escalating, especially when the political goals of all the parties involved are limited. If there are any doubts concerning the willingness or capability to intervene, the probability of entering the military campaign phase will increase distinctly. Priority should be always given to the goal of influencing the enemy's calculation not to make use of his warfare capability: either by stressing one's own convincing military superiority or by providing the enemy positive incentives to forgo force. If used cleverly, both elements can complement each other.

Especially in the case of "small wars," when the state has disintegrated or social, economic and government structures have to be rebuilt, new capabilities are required in the area of "nation-building," the forces notably being needed to support consolidation. Nongovernmental and governmental protagonists will develop new fields of action in the course of asymmetric warfare. These will include: urban areas, the information area, the international media world, the different areas of social, economic and political life and perhaps even outer space. As already stated for the security policy parameters, every form of risk potential in societies and all forms of transition from non-violent to violent action—e.g. guerilla action, terrorism, intifada, organized crime, migration, piracy, etc.—can be instrumentalized militarily. Especially urban areas, which will probably grow considerably in the decades to come, offer the protagonists a wide range of possibilities to use organized force and thus wage war in the gray area of organized crime with considerable financial backing—e.g. the drug mafia has an estimated annual turnover of approximately 500 billion U.S. dollars.

Consequently, the military elements of post-industrial societies or the security elements of the future should be designed as follows:

- command and control:

  interconnected complex of command and control, communications and information collection and processing as well as intelligence (C4ISR) at the disposal of the political and military leaders as well as an adequate logistics set-up for all task elements used.

- forward-based elements:

  small modular task groups with a high C2 capability, the necessary situation picture, access to land-, air- and sea-based active options as well as strategic-operational mobility.

- force multipliers and stand-off elements:

  land-, air- and sea-based active systems which ensure that decisions can be brought about in a stand-off manner with or without the support of the forward-based task elements.

- consolidation elements:

  militarily organized and armed police or similar units with components for nation-building, economic and social intervention as well as for countering international criminality/terrorism. This includes experts from the areas of administration, social affairs, infrastructure, judiciary, civil defense, etc., as well as possibly support from and cooperation with non-governmental organizations.

All these elements must be able to participate in multinational coalition operations. Besides a small number of major nations, there will be few states left capable of waging an interstate war with any prospect of success. This is in stark contrast to the emergence of more and more new and non-governmental protagonists prepared to wage war. But this is the rationale of warfare: While modern industrial states are interested in preventing war out of self-interest, there are states and non-governmental protagonists which use war as an economic or ideological factor leading to another cost-benefit calculation. Furthermore, information warfare offers the possibility to have a considerable effect, especially on those protagonists which depend on command and control systems and employ them hierarchically.

While the military campaign is increasingly waged from a distance, the implementation of the political goals calls for forces on the ground. Based on the existing conflict analysis, these goals must as a rule include capabilities enabling them to win the hearts and minds of the societies concerned. In this type of operation, military power has the dual purpose of stopping the leaders of failing states who are ready to use force and of helping to promote the stable development of a region by supporting political, social and economic development. This requires the build-up of a wide range of elements of self-organized units within these societies. So purely military approaches are just as likely to fail as wholly civilian ones if the exclusive right to use force is devolved too early to the interplay of regional actors. But the exclusive right to use military power in a region is primarily a question of internal safety, i.e., the use of force and the adequacy of means, such as police and police clearing-up methods. Cooperation between the military, the police and other political-social forces has to be reconsidered.

As threats can arise within a minimum of time without any warning, hitting states and societies alike, it will be particularly important to react quickly both to deter and to reduce acute threats. This notably includes employing an effective intelligence and information system as well as decision-making instruments at the political and military level. Moreover, the readiness and mobility of the existing forces have to be increased. The military capabilities have to support preventive offensive options against possible protagonists to counter threats to Europe, but also to countries beyond the European borders. Such capabilities increase the deterrent character of the armed forces and can possibly save lives as well. This applies in particular against the background of asymmetric risks.

Getting there

To this end, the European Union needs to re-focus its foreign and security policy—at least the core of the ESDP, the Petersberg tasks. Rescue and humanitarian operations, peacekeeping and the role of combat troops in peacemaking mean very different things today compared to what the limited concept of 1992 envisioned when the Petersberg tasks were announced. The world has moved on and so European defense needs to move on, too.

There are currently over two million people under arms in the European NATO countries, compared to only 1.4 million in the U.S. But very few EU countries possess armed forces with a power projection capability. Flexibility through modularity, sustainability, strategic and tactical mobility and firepower are key characteristics of a transformed force capable of meeting tomorrow's threats—features that are seldom found in Europe. Alone forty main categories of shortfalls have been identified in the European Capability Action Plan—a plan that focuses more on today's needs instead of tomorrow's.

For operations at the top end of the Petersberg task spectrum, military air and sea transport assets and capabilities need to be considerably reinforced. Force sustainability and survivability require a reinforced logistics capacity to support troops once they have been deployed and improved capabilities for establishing supply lines. Search and rescue capabilities need to be improved to allow a hostile environment to be covered. Europe's lack of capabilities is fed by redundancies among European forces, a lack of co-ordination between European defense industries, and armed forces trained predominantly for territorial defense.

These very facts underline the fact that there is little point in establishing another heavy corps-sized force similar to NATO's Rapid Reaction Corps. What Europeans really need is a limited number of rapidly deployable special forces, specialized forces, and force multipliers of strategic value. The goal must be to transform Europe's militaries into forces that can successfully meet 21st century security challenges. This requires:

- closing the technology gap and even passing over it wherever possible by developing front-end technologies and capabilities,

- specializing in a limited number of specific capabilities and

- sustaining commitment to co-operability, both among the forces of EU states and with the U.S.

The war in Afghanistan has once again demonstrated the utility of immediate reaction special forces and forces equipped for multiple-intensity peacekeeping/peacemaking missions ranging from short-duration peace support operations in high-risk environments to long-duration peace support operations in low to medium–risk environments. Given the nature of the emerging risks, Europe could produce an elite number of special forces relatively easily and back them up with sufficient specialized forces and peacekeepers to meet most short to medium-term operational requirements. A re-focusing of ESDP should also stretch to deployability and sustainability and power projection capability.

The creation of a European small, but well equipped and trained "spearhead force" in particular, composed of land, sea and air elements, appears to be an attractive concept. Being kept at a high level of readiness for deployment in response to unfolding crises, it would provide the EU with an important, effective instrument. It would also constitute an additional asset for NATO operations and consequently drastically increase Europe's political weight in Washington. Some European nations already have high-readiness elements among their expeditionary capability. These national forces could be easily earmarked for European operations and their readiness levels declared to Europe.

A second component might be high-readiness elements of existing multinational European formations such as the EUROCORPS. Yet, it would not be sufficient to rely on the development of a truly multinational capability to meet the spearhead force requirement as it needs to be of a modular nature and comprise a number of national and multinational force elements. Multinational operations are likely to remain the task of coalitions of the willing, with the availability of forces likely to be dependent on the commitment of the contributing nations. Yet common training and readiness standards, including an underlying common doctrine would provide additional benefits.

As the Europeans lag behind the Americans—not because there is a technology gap, but because there is a lack of determination—they also need to harmonize their forces better, to make more efficient and more economic use of their defense investments. More than being a matter of money, Europe's present defense deficiencies have to do with a lack of national will and institutional effectiveness. Too often in the past, with the Balkans as a striking example, Europe has been unable to respond with the efficiency or timeliness that developments in the real world demand. National will needs to yield the necessary funds for common security. On top of all that, the money needs to be spent more effectively than in the past, as well as on the modern systems that are required to meet the new risks in a changed security environment rather than on systems whose principal function appears to be to preserve jobs and duplicate U.S. systems. It is therefore important to strengthen intra-European military co-operation. The necessary progress could be realized more easily if leading European allies focused and integrated their efforts to transform their forces. Europe should seek to make in quality what it lacks in quantity, by ensuring efficient spending, but also by adopting a dedicated transformation program focused on strategic shortcomings.

In sum, Europe's present focus on improving and pooling capabilities needs to be broadened to transformation and also include Euro-Atlantic co-operability, particularly in the more challenging part of the mission spectrum. Consequently, ESDP should have not just one military purpose but two: 1) stability operations with or without the United States and 2) advanced expeditionary warfare with the United States. The former would be mainly for contingencies in and near Europe, while the latter could be for contingencies anywhere in the world where U.S. and European common interests are threatened.

The transatlantic dimension

Getting a significant European transformation process started will ensure that strategic doctrines remain compatible across the Atlantic. There is much talk about the transatlantic technology gap. Less attention is being paid to the differences that persist among the U.S. and European countries about the use of armed forces, particularly with regard to power projection and expeditionary warfare. This process should go hand in hand with mechanisms designed to adapt priorities in capability development and improvement, including the necessary interface with NATO.

Of course, a certain contradiction between Washington's demand for improved military capabilities on the one hand and its anxiety about losing influence on the other has yet to be overcome. This requires the development of a *transatlantic security and defense identity*, instead of just a "narrow" European one.[7] The protection of their worldwide interests calls for Europe to sustain a political, financial and military commitment. For its part, the U.S. should bear in mind that since the international system is prone to crises, the future intervention force of the EU will be a source of support for NATO and will thus add value to the transatlantic relationship.

Hopefully, it will also increase the opportunities for transatlantic co-operation in the design and procurement of new arms systems.

Armaments policy, including defense research and development, has remained essentially the playground of national prerogatives. Strategic considerations and economic interests have combined in a mutually reinforcing process that perpetuated fragmentation and dispersion of efforts and a weakening of the competitiveness of the European defense industry. Europeans will have to get their act together if they want to achieve a better position to engage in more effective and mutually beneficial transatlantic industrial and technological co-operation. The U.S. will have to respond by being more open towards sharing technology and know-how with allies.

The relationship between NATO and the European Union over the past decades can best be described as two major entities existing side by side but failing to share many responsibilities. The militarily and politically strong and capable North Atlantic Treaty Organization dealt mainly with security and defense issues regarding the Euro-Atlantic region, while the economically strong European Union vested its interest primarily in the economic growth and social well-being of the European continent. During the past fifty years, Europe has been repeatedly urged to bear a larger part of the defense burden. The U.S. has regularly asked the Europeans to strengthen the "European pillar" of the North Atlantic Alliance.

As Europe is fundamentally changing, it is now developing a stronger defense capability. The once loose collection of states has become a union of unprecedented economic and political strength. With the gross domestic product of the European Union roughly equivalent to that of the United States, it is approaching a credible defense dimension in order to collaborate politically and militarily with their transatlantic partners in the prevention of conflicts and the management of crises on a fair burden-sharing basis. The increase in the Europeans' capacity to act and to project European power will provide the foundations for a viable long-term partnership—a goal pursued by Europeans and Americans alike. Close co-operation and transparency would certainly strengthen the partnership as well as the ability to manage crises more effectively. But all of this is closely related to the success of the European security venture—the building of a European Union with nations that acquire the capabilities, develop the organization, and sustain the will to manage future crises and conflicts, if need be by projecting European power.

Notes:

1. Javier Solana, *Europe: Security in the Twenty-First Century*, The Olof Palme Memorial Lecture, Stockholm, 20 June 2001, paragraph 28.

2. See Bundeswehr Center for Analyses and Studies, *Streitkräfte, Fähigkeiten und Technologie im 21. Jahrhundert*, Waldbröl, 30 September 2002, on which this analysis is based.

3. See Paul Collier, "Economic Causes of Civil Conflict and their Implications for Policy," 2000 (http://www.reliefweb.int/library/documents/civilconflict.pdf) and Peter Lock, "Ökonomien des Krieges," 2001 (http://www.peter-lock.de/texte/Kriegs%9Akonomien2.html).

4. See Paul Kennedy, *The Rise and Fall of the Great Powers: Economic Change and Military Conflict from 1500 to 2000*, New York: Vintage Books, 1989.

5. See Ernst-Otto Czempiel, "Eine neue Ordnung für Europa," *International Politics and Society*, no. 4/1998 (http://www.fes.de/ipg/ipg4_98/artczempiel.html).

6. Javier Solana, *Report on the Middle East to the Göteborg European Council*, 15 June 2001.

7. See Holger H. Mey, *Deutsche Sicherheitspolitik 2030*, Frankfurt am Main/Bonn: Report Verlag, 2001, p. 93.

ESDP and International Stability

Russia's Role in the ESDP

Tuomas Forsberg

Russia's role in the ESDP is like the hound of Baskerville in the famous Sherlock Holmes story; it is interesting precisely because it does not bark. Economics lies at the heart of EU-Russia cooperation, not security and defense. The EU member states have not developed the ESDP with the Russia threat—or its assets, for that matter—in mind and the existing links between the ESDP and Russia are tenuous. Russia does not figure in the EU's military threat images but neither is Russia regarded as a valuable partner that could help construct and strengthen ESDP. For some individual member states and especially for some candidates, Russia may still loom as a potential threat, but such thinking has not found its way from those capitals to Brussels. Russia, for its part, has welcomed the ESDP but it has not quite made its mind about it. In Russia's relations with the EU, EU enlargement and especially the encirclement of the Kaliningrad region are seen as posing a bigger threat than the ESDP.

The non-salience of Russia's role in the ESDP and the lack of strategic visions is perplexing given the historical importance of Russia for European security, the ever-present geographic proximity, tight political relations at the highest level and the present largely overlapping threat images in Brussels and Moscow. Yet, there are a number of reasons for the present situation. Among them are the significance of the United States as the primary security partner, sheer ignorance of each other, and bureaucratic inertia, as well as differences in the strategic culture and values. Nevertheless, in the longer run, it will be both impossible and sub-optimal to continue developing the ESDP without a closer relationship with Moscow. Both the changing global strategic landscape and EU enlargement towards Russian borders will dictate that.

Most current reflections on the relationship between the EU and Russia suggest that Russia also should be an important partner for the EU in the field of security. There are very few people, who resist such a vision publicly. Although the achievements so far are rather limited, the trend in the relationship is clear. Javier Solana has argued that "the strategic partnership between the EU and Russia is of fundamental importance —, but its full bene fits have yet to be realized." He sees "many reasons why Russia could become an even closer partner with the EU in the future."[1] In Chris Patten's view Russia is naturally a key partner also in security cooperation.[2] The same view is sustained by a number of independent analysts. Michael Emerson, for example, suggests that strategic partnership becomes the name of the game, although it will take time to develop it.[3] Graeme Herd thinks the key dynamics that shape the international politics in the longer run suggest that Russia's future lies to the West and can be anchored by EU military co-operation.[4]

In this article, I will first examine the mutual perceptions of the EU and Russia and then look into the development of the security relationship between the EU and Russia. After that, I will discuss the reasons for the present state of affairs in more detail and go through three different explanations of why Russia's role in the ESDP has been limited. Finally, I will conclude by assessing the prospects for future security cooperation between the EU and Russia.

The EU view of Russia

The threat that the Soviet Union used to be to the Europeans no longer dominates European view of Russia. The idea of a "residual threat" of Russia was part of discussions in NATO in the early 1990s, but it was gradually replaced by other concerns. The view that Russia does not pose any threat to Europe has actually given a boost to a more Europeanized NATO and thereby to the ESDP. In the view of most Europeans, Russia is weakened and it has so many problems of its own that it cannot afford a military conflict with the West. The EU has seen Russia as a source of instability, in particular in mid-1990s, but at the turn of the millennium even the fears of major chaos in Russia influencing the security of the EU disappeared into the margins.

During the 1990s and into the beginning of the 21st century, the major concern was the instability in Eastern Europe and especially in the Balkans. From the perspective of Brussels, the instability in the Mediterranean area has always been seen as more signi ficant than the one in Russia. Moreover, and especially after September 11, the threats are more diffuse and more dif ficult to de fine by geographical terms as the sources are not particular states but terrorist organizations and other criminal groups.[5]

From the perspective of the EU, there is a clear difference between Central and Eastern European countries and Russia. In contrast to the view of Central and Eastern European countries, the EU does not foresee accession of Russia into the Union. The goal is to bind Russia to European values and norms, without, however, offering a membership. Although the strategy of stabilization is largely the same, in its policies vis-à-vis Russia the EU lacks its most effective tool.

Neither does Russia nor its nearby areas figure highly in most visions about where the EU rapid reaction force could be deployed. The Balkans and especially the Kosovo crisis triggered the launch of the ESDP and that area has dominated its operationalization, too. In discussions about possible future operations the Mediterranean area and even Africa have mentioned more often than areas closer to Russia. Only recently more attention has been paid to Moldova and Caucasus, and since September 11 to Central Asia.

Although the EU regards Russia as a potential partner, it does not see its military and defense policy as a pattern to follow. The main reference point for Europeans when building up the ESDP is the United States, not Russia. For this reason, there is little desire to learn from Russian experiences or buy Russian military technology. The interests of the EU in developing the security relationship with Russia lie most clearly in practical crisis management cooperation. In particular, EU could possibly need Russian transport aircraft to provide strategic lift for its rapid reaction forces. Yet, there are doubts whether Russian assets could really help fill in the EU's gaps in capabilities.[6]

Russian view of the EU

For Russians, the EU has had a much more positive image than has NATO, which the Russians see as an institution founded to counter Moscow. Whereas Russia used to object NATO expansion, it welcomed the EU enlargement and it did not object when even former Soviet republics like the Baltic states were joining it. EU's positive image partly depended on its civilian character, but also its emerging and increasing security role received more positive than negative judgments in Moscow. Not even the nomination of NATO's Secretary

General Javier Solana to be the High Representative of the Common Foreign and Security Policy changed Russia's basically af firmative view of the EU.[7]

In principle, Russians could see ESDP as a risk. Given Russia's historical experience of Napoleon's and Hitler's invasions of Russia, an emergence of an enlarging and more uni fied European power with a military dimension, should ring alarm bells. Yet, apart from a few people, it is dif ficult to find indication that the EU had penetrated Russian calculations of military risks. Russian military documents, such as the National Security Blueprint and its new military doctrine that was adopted in 2000, indicate that the EU does not constitute a threat to Russia. In both documents, the EU is present by its absence. Dmitry Danilov has argued that even high-level generals did not see the ESDP as posing a threat to Russia.[8] By contrast, Russian security assessment is to a signi ficant degree similar to that of the EU, seeing most risks in failed states and regions in the south and paying also attention to soft security threats.

Some Russian analysts and of ficials working on European integration have a more negative view of the EU. Yet, this negative view is based on issues other than security and defense, namely EU anti-dumping measures, its criticism of the war in Chechnya, the implications of enlargement for trade and border-crossings. The issue of Kaliningrad developed into a major problem in the Russian-EU relations during 2001-2002, but the problem has been dealt with as a "soft" security issue rather than as a "hard" security challenge. However, a more negative assessment on the ESDP comes from Stanislav Tkatchenko, who sees the ESDP rather cynically and thinks that "objectively speaking, Russia should react to military cooperation within the European Union negatively."[9]

Most Russian analysts view the ESDP positively, partly because it does not mean a common European defense and because its focus is on the softer end of military operations. Yet Russians still prefer, at least ideally, a European security system that is based on the UN and OSCE rather than on the EU, because Russia is and will not become a EU member.[10] Although Russia's view is positive, military cooperation with the EU has been not been very high on the agenda. Russia's concrete interests in developing the security relationship with the EU have been more on the military industrial side than in joint crisis management.

Current achievements

The cornerstone of the EU–Russia relationship is the Partnership and Cooperation Agreement that was signed in 1994 and entered into force in 1997. The main objective of the agreement is the establishment of a common free trade area but it also calls for a more intensified political dialogue between the EU and Russia. However, when the PCA agreement was signed, the EU did not have any visible plans of its defense dimension.

Another central EU document concerning its relationship with Russia was the Common Strategy of the European Union on Russia that was accepted by the European Council in 1999. The strategy outlines a variety of means that support the aim of consolidating democracy, market economics and the rule of law in Russia. The EU wants to strengthen political dialogue with Russia. As far as cooperation in the field of security is concerned, the EU expresses its will to continue "cooperation with Russia in the elaboration of aspects of the European Security Charter." The strategy paper also includes the idea of "facilitating the participation of Russia when the EU avails itself of the WEU for missions of the range within the Petersberg tasks."[11]

Russia's response to the EU common strategy on Russia was its Medium-term Strategy for the Development of Relations between the Russian Federation and the European Union that was adopted in October 1999. Russia had not, and it could not, take any de finitive stance to the emerging defense dimension of the EU, but it was viewed positively, particularly because it matched Russians' idea of a multipolar world. The Russian's formulation of the strategy was seen as a step forward in Brussels and most member states. Europeans relieved that the ESDP did not seem to provoke the Russians, although most of them did not want to subscribe to the Russian view that it will "counterbalance NATO-centrism" in Europe.

Since 1999, ESDP related issues have been regularly discussed at the EU-Russia biannual summit meetings. A brief overview of the summits shows how the relationship has developed during the past three years.

At the May 2000 Summit in Moscow, Russian President Vladimir Putin signaled that Russia was very interested in cooperation in the field of security and defense, but the Russian position was still conditional. Russians had studied carefully the conclusions of the Helsinki summit and they seemed to pay particular attention to the question of whether the EU was willing and capable to act militarily without an OSCE or UN mandate. For Russians the important yardstick with which they judged the ESDP was, in the aftermath of NATO's war on Yugoslavia, whether the policy was based on the principles of international law and the UN charter. If that would be the case, Russia would be ready for close interaction.[12]

The summit meeting in Paris in October 2000 was an important landmark in forming the security relationship between the EU and Russia, because then Russia had formed a positive opinion on the ESDP. The joint statement of the summit welcomed "the progress achieved in the common European security and defense policy," with the addendum that its objective is "to contribute effectively to crisis management in compliance with United Nations principles." The parties also decided to strengthen cooperation in the field of security with intensifying dialogue at various levels and examine mechanisms for a Russian contribution to the European Union's crisis management operations.[13]

Crisis management and enhancing mutual contacts were the most important items discussed at the next Russia–EU Summit in May 2001. The joint statement of the summit identi fied "crisis management in Europe as well as UN and OSCE matters — as important areas of co-operation." Moreover, the parties attempted at tightening communication links. It was agreed that the EU will inform Russia on developments in ESDP matters and Russia will inform the EU on the development of its security and defense policy and its implementation within the fora for political dialogue.[14]

The mechanism about how to improve mutual contacts was the main result of the October 2001 EU-Russia summit that was held in Brussels. The EU and Russia agreed on monthly consultations with the Political and Security Committee troika and Russian representatives, mainly the Russian ambassador to the EU. It is noteworthy that out of all third powers, Russia was the first with which the EU agreed on such a mechanism of consultations. Otherwise the summit meeting was shaped by the views that the global war on terrorism renders the EU-Russian security relationship more important than before.

The security cooperation between the EU and Russia was developed into a more concrete direction at the May 2002 summit in Moscow. The EU and Russia identi fied key areas of cooperation including the use of Russian long-haul air transportation to provide strategic lift for ESDP operations and Russian participation in the EU Police Mission in Bosnia and Herzegovina. To facilitate information exchange, a decision was made to appoint a Russian contact person with the EU Military Staff.

Although these achievements show a progressive movement in the relations between the EU and Russia, a closer examination of the relationship reveals a number of problems. The relationship is not as close and smooth as one could imagine. One example of the problems is that half a year after the summit decision, a Russian contact person at the EU military staff has not been nominated. Also the exchange of information has remained restricted. We may therefore want to ask, what explains the relatively slow progress in the relationship.

The Primacy of the United States

One possible reason that explains why the EU and Russia have been moving rather cautiously when developing their mutual security relationship is that for both Europeans and Russians their primary security relationship is the one with the United States. Although some may wish to strengthen the ESDP in order to balance the power of the United States, most Europeans see that the ESDP as a means add to that power and to rejuvenate the transatlantic relationship. Moreover, Americans would not necessarily see anything bad in Russian participation in the ESDP, if that would contribute to a larger stability in Europe.[15] Yet, many Europeans may fear that closer cooperation with Russia would give a signal to Washington that they are no longer needed in Europe. In Dmitry Danilov's view the EU is hesitant because it does not want to "risk jeopardizing the NATO/U.S. supportive attitude towards ESDP by excessive rapprochement with Moscow."[16]

It has been assumed that for Russia, the ESDP was instrumental in its attempt to balance the United States and break up the "hegemony" of NATO in the same way as Moscow was seen playing the European card during the Cold War. Especially in the aftermath of the NATO enlargement and the war on Kosovo, Russia tried to find alternative ways to influence security. If NATO enlargement was perceived as a setback because Russia's voice was not adequately heard, NATO's warfare without UN mandate caused an even stronger shock in Moscow. A strong EU with an emerging military dimension would add a new star in the security constellation. Russia followed closely the development of the ESDP and cherished hopes that it could lead to multipolar world and a weakened NATO, but the process turned out to be a disappointment from the point of view Russia. The EU Summit in Nice in December 2000 underlined the close linkage between the EU and NATO rather than the EU's autonomous role that was more visible in the Cologne declaration half a year earlier. Russians felt that European states would ultimately side with the U.S. on most security related issues. Russia shifted its grand strategy and concluded that Washington is the key to influence the developments. Consequently, the ESDP was now seen more as a means to approach Washington than a factor that counterbalances it.[17]

Russia's improved relationship with the United States has decreased its interest towards the ESDP. Although Putin might be a European at heart, his head seems to be Atlanticist. Putin has understood and accepted that the ESDP will remain in the shadow of NATO for some time, and for Russia it is more important to influence NATO than ESDP. The idea of decoupling Europeans from America is no longer a priority to Moscow.

The irony is that at the same time when Russia is less willing to play the European card, the transatlantic relationship seems to be drifting apart for its own reasons. Despite the solidarity that the Europeans showed in the aftermath of the September 11, they have different ideas about how the war on terror should be fought. Yet, so far the problems in the transatlantic relationship have not made Russia more attractive to the EU. Although Europeans have started to be increasingly concerned about American unilateralism, they have not been willing to adopt a balancing strategy against Washington.

Ignorance and Bureaucratic Inertia

Another reason that may explain the slow pro file of the security relationship between the EU and Russia is the sheer ignorance and the bureaucratic sluggishness in developing the cooperation. In particular, it has been often noted that Russians do not know much about the European Union. This applies not only to public opinion but also to the foreign policy elite. Margot Light, John Löwenhardt and Stephen White found out in their interviews that even those who should have been better informed seemed to lack "even elementary knowledge about the EU."[18]

Vladimir Baranovsky identi fies two main reasons to the lack of knowledge about the EU. Firstly, most of the attention of the elite and the public in Russia between the mid-1980s and mid-1990s was focused on the dramatic domestic changes in Russia. Against that background, developments in the EU did not seem that important for Russia. Secondly, Russian foreign policy had suffered from illusions with respect to the Western institutions in the early 1990s. As a consequence, Russians were suspicious about closer cooperation with the EU as well.[19]

Furthermore, Russia may have had dif ficulty in understanding the role of EU in security and defense because of its traditional focus on power and nation-states in international politics. In hard security questions, Russians still believed, and perhaps rightly so, that capitals mattered much more than Brussels. This perspective was only strengthened by the dif ficulties to find a common European position to the possible war on Iraq. As the ESDP has not yet become very concrete, it has been logical for Russians to adopt a wait and see approach, although some Russian analysts have argued that Russia would have better chances to influence the process because it is in its formative phase.

At the same time, the development of the relationship has been difficult for the EU as well also because of reasons of ignorance and bureaucratic sluggishness. Knowledge on Russia has not been the traditional strengths of the EU external relations. When the common security and defense policy was only emerging, it was just too dif ficult to think what the implications were for relations with Russia. As Francois Heisbourg has noted, the development of the EU has been possible only because it has remained ambiguous and most controversial questions have been avoided.[20] The EU should first develop the ESDP and then see how it can be accommodated with third powers. Regarding the role of the third powers, sorting out the relationship with Turkey has to be solved first. The EU representatives have announced that the dialogue on the ESDP will be conducted in the light of progress made by the EU, which means that Russia will have to wait that internal disputes have been settled. One does not want to put the cart before the horse.

Russia's role in the ESDP has remained ambiguous, because of the EU's dif ficulties making its long term policy towards Russia more con- crete. Although the EU has adopted a common strategy on Russia, it is not very helpful in guiding the EU's policy choices. The strategy paper was criticized by the Secretary General of the EU Council Javier Solana, because it was too loose and inde finite.[21] It was more a shopping list of different means or a declaration of purpose rather than a strategy that identi fied concrete steps that were needed in order to achieve larger visions. Moreover, it was a typical "fair weather strategy" that did not entail policy recommendations that could be adopted when things went wrong, which has not helped the development of the ESDP.

Strategic Culture and Values

A third main reason that may impede closer relationship between the EU and Russia in security and defense is their different strategic culture and values. Heinz Timmermann has argued that the develop- ment of cooperation between EU and Russia depends on increasing compatibility in the areas of democracy, human rights, economic order and international relations.[22] Alexander Rahr has made the point that the EU is reluctant to open genuine security dialogue with Russia, because it perceives the value gap being too wide.[23]

Values are an important part of the European Union's identity and it has made a strong commitment to foster its values of democracy, human rights, market economy and rule of law. This is evident in the strategy paper on Russia: "EU welcomes Russia's return to its rightful place in the European family in the spirit of friendship, cooperation, fair accom- modation of interests and on the foundations of shared values enshrined in the common heritage of European civilization." In other words, val- ues are at the heart of the EU's relationship with Russia. Yet, EU does not accept that Russia fully subscribes to those values. Values, strategic culture and practices related to the use of military force are different.

The value gap became most visible due to the war in Chechnya. European Union leaders criticized Russian government for its exces- sive use of military force and the TACIS program was frozen. The criticism was dampened down after September 11, but it did not alter European views about the deficits in Russian human rights culture. Most European governments would be subject to allegations that they were helping to suppress minorities if they started close military cooperation with Russia. Moreover, Europeans may feel that Russia has no other rational choice than to cooperate with Europe and therefore there is no need to compromise on values.

Yet, it is important to bear in mind that the values gap between the EU and Russia is most visible on human rights issues. On many other questions of international politics, the EU member states are actually closer to Russia than to the U.S. as can be demonstrated by a look at UN voting behavior. Nevertheless, the human rights issues are important enough sustain the traditional perception that there are differences between EU and Russian value systems.

Closing the gap?

Within the limits of this short article, it is impossible to say exactly how much the different factors affect the development of the EU-Russia security relationship. It is also unclear what their impact will be in the future. The transatlantic relationship is in a state of ferment and the Europeans struggle with getting the ESDP fully operationalized. We see many factors that push the EU and Russia closer together, but also some areas that may diminish the need for cooperation. For example, when EU has its own capability for strategic lift, Russia may seem less attractive as a partner.

Anyway, as several factors explain the relative non-salience of the EU–Russia security relationship, there are no simple tricks how to improve it. Observers have noticed that the relationship between the EU and Russia has fallen short of expectations partly because it has been guided more by visions than concrete steps. Both the EU and Russia have a culture that revolves around speeches and documents. Therefore analysts have suggested that the EU and Russia should focus on practical long term cooperation instead of producing joint declarations. In view of Sergei Karaganov, the problem is that the EU-Russia dialogue is more a bureaucratic exercise than a vehicle for further integration and it may therefore lead to disillusionment. As a consequence, Karaganov claims, Russia may search for allies and opportunities elsewhere.[24] Michael Emerson argues that achieving a convergence of ideologies will be difficult, but the parties must adopt the strategy of learning by doing. The events of September 11 provide potentially an epoch-making situation that can help to overcome psychological obstacles.[25] Stephan de Spiegeleire warns against drawing conclusions too hastily. In his view, it is unclear whether Europe can or even should reciprocate to Putin's new openings. Spiegeleire's argument is that the relationship with Russia is too important to be left hostage to the conjunction of various impulses.[26]

Security cooperation in the nearby areas, actual and potential conflict spots between the EU and Russia, will provide a concrete challenge for the relationship. Where and when might such cooperation take place? As of now, the EU and Russia have not discussed any concrete plans, and there seems to be no congruence between the views of analysts. The conflict areas that Michael Emerson particularly regards as possible cases for joint operations are Moldova and the Caucasus. Dmitri Trenin, in turn, could foresee peacekeeping operations in Abkhazia and Nagorno-Karabakh, whereas Stanislav Tkachenko sees it hardly possible that the EU would participate in crisis management in the CIS area, because it is Russian traditional sphere of interest. The only area where EU and Russia have common interests is the Balkans, but when Russia is losing influence there, military cooperation with the EU would benefit the EU more than Russia.[27] Graeme Herd, in turn, suggests that one could start military cooperation in areas that are located further away, such as in the Middle East, and then work together in a closer region.[28] Finally, Europe should not merely think about how Russia should join its operations, but also how it could contribute to Russian defense. Julian Lindley-French suggests that in the future there might be occasions when Russia could play the role of a lead nation in military operation to which EU countries may want to join.[29]

In the rapidly changing global landscape, there are a number of security issues that the EU and Russia can and should address together. Although the trend is to put emphasis on practical cooperation, it would be too easy to dismiss the importance of talk and common visions. Visions that remain unfulfilled can lead to disillusionment, but if they do not exist or if they are not developed in the first place, that can cause disappointment as well.

Notes:

1. Javier Solana, "The EU-Russia Relationship at the Start of the Millennium," Kommersant, http://ue.eu.int/solana (29 August 2002).

2. Chris Patten, speech at the European Business Club (EBC) Conference on Shaping Russian-European Integration in the 21st Century, Moscow, 28 may 2002, http://europa.eu.int/comm/external_relations/news/patten/sp02_235.htm

3. Michael Emerson, *The Elephant and the Bear. The European Union, Russia and their Near Abroads* (Brussels: Center for European Policy Studies, 2001).

4. Graeme Herd , "Russia and the European Union," in Charles Jenkins—Julie Smith (eds.), *Through the Paper Curtain: Insiders and Outsiders in the New Europe* (London: Blackwells, forthcoming).

5. Henrik Larsen, "The Discourse on the EU's Role in the World," in Birthe Hansen—Bertel Heurlin, *The New World Order: Contrasting Theories* (Basingstoke: Palgrave, 2000), pp. 217-244.

6. Mark Webber, "Third-Party Inclusion in the European Security and Defense Policy. A Case Study of Russia," *European Foreign Affairs Review*, vol. 6, no. 4, 2001, pp. 409-426.

7. Dieter Mahncke, "Russia's Attitude to the European Security and Defense Policy," *European Foreign Affairs Review*, vol. 6, no. 4, 2001, pp. 427-436.

8. Dmitry Danilov, "The EU's Rapid Reaction Capabilities: A Russian Perspective," prepared for the IISS/CEPS European Security Forum, 10 September 2001, http://www.eusec.org/danilov.htm (23 August 2002).

9. Stanislav Tkachenko, "The EU's Crisis Management from the Russian Perspective," in Graeme Herd—Jouko Huru (eds.), *EU Civilian Crisis Management*. M22 (Camberley: Conflict Studies Research Center, The Royal Military Academy Sandhurst, 2001).

10. Andrei Zagorski, "Sicherheitspolitischer Dialog Russland—EU: Hintergründe, Entwicklungen, Grenzen," in Hans-George Erhards (ed.), *Die Europäische Sicherheits- und Verteidigungspolitik. Positionen, Perzeptionen, Probleme, Perspektiven* (Baden-Baden: Nomos, 2002), pp. 193-205.

11. See Hiski Haukkala and Sergei Medvedev (eds), The EU Common Strategy on Russia. Learning the Grammar of the CFSP *Programme on the Northern Dimension of the CFSP* no. 11 (Helsinki: Finnish Institute of International Affairs, 2001).

12. Press Release, Russian Ministry of Foreign Affairs, 29 June 2000.

13. Joint Statement of Russia—EU Summit, Paris 30 October, 2001. http://ue.eu.int/newsroom/

14. Joint Statement of Russia—EU Summit, Moscow 17 May 2001. http://ue.eu.int/newsroom/

15. Angela Stent, "An American View on Russian Security Policy and EU— Russian Relations," *European Security Forum Working Paper* No. 6 (Center for European Policy Studies & International Institute for Strategic Studies, March 2002).

16. Danilov, "The EU's Rapid Reaction Capabilities: A Russian Perspective," p. 4.

17. Dmitrios Triantaphyllou, "The EU and Russia: A Security Partnership," Seminar Memo, European Union Institute for Security Studies, Paris, 25 March 2002.

18. Margot Light, John Löwenhardt and Stephen White, "Russian Perspectives on European Security," *European Foreign Affairs Review*, vol. 5, no. 4, 2000, pp. 489-505.

19. Vladimir Baranovsky, Russia's Attitude Towards the EU: Political Aspects. *Programme on the Northern Dimension of the CFSP* no. 15 (Helsinki: Finnish Institute of International Affairs, 2002).

20. Francois Heisbourg, "Europe's Strategic Ambitions: The Limits of Ambiguity," *Survival* vol. 42, no. 2, 2000, pp. 5-15.

21. Bulletin Quotidien Europe 2228, 31 January 2001.

22. Heinz Timmermann, "European-Russian Partnership: What Future?," *European Foreign Affairs Review* vol. 5, no. 2, 2000, pp. 165-174.

23. Alexander Rahr, "EU View on Putin's Foreign Policy," http://www.dgap. org/english/text/rahr_columbia.html (23 August 2002).

24. Sergei Karaganov, "Building Bridges with Brussels," *Financial Times*, 18 May 2001.

25. Emerson, *The Elephant and the Bear*, p. 4.

26. Stephan de Spiegeleire, "Europe's Security Relationship with Russia: Staying the Course," *European Security Forum Working Paper* No. 6 (Center for European Policy Studies & International Institute for Strategic Studies, March 2002).

27. Stanislav Tkachenko, "The EU's Crisis Management from the Russian Perspective," p. 56.

28. Herd, "Russia and the European Union."

29. Julian Lindley-French, "Terms of Engagement. The Paradox of American Power and the Transatlantic Dilemma post-11 September," *Chaillot Papers* no. 52 (Paris: European Union Institute for Security Studies, 2002), p. 71.

ESDP and International Peacekeeping

Esther Brimmer

The end of the Cold War, increasing globalization, and the September 11 terrorist attacks have changed the landscape of international security. World leaders versed in the high-politics of strategic affairs are finding that they have to grapple with complex humanitarian emergencies, intra-national conflict, and asymmetrical threats from terrorists. Even a low intensity festering conflicts can have a large international impact if it generates refugees, disease, and terrorists. The location or severity of a conflict can elicit widespread international attention. Throughout the 1990s, policymakers in North America, Europe, and elsewhere tangled with a variety of complex conflicts that often necessitated drawing together emergency relief, military assets, and diplomatic coalitions. The new security threats demand new combinations of foreign policy assets. The European Union presents itself as a comprehensive security organization able to field a full range of foreign policy tools, and, hence, would seem to have access to the resources needed to address these complex problems.

This chapter explores the extent to which the evolving European Security and Defense Policy enables the European Union to make a significant contribution to international peace and security particularly in the areas of peacekeeping, conflict prevention, and post-conflict security. The chapter will begin with an analysis of conflict prevention and management, then will present the EU's policies and will examine the contribution of ESDP. The chapter will conclude with a comparison of EU and U.S. approaches to conflict prevention and management and the implications of their views for the transatlantic relationship.

Conflict Prevention and Management

The fight against terrorism has cast a new light on post-conflict reconstruction. Although the Bush administration has been wary of "nation-building," the U.S.-led anti-terrorism campaign led to the end of the Taliban regime in Kabul. Helping establish a new government has put the United States and the international community in the middle of a complex post-conflict reconstruction effort. Europeans play key roles in that reconstruction and provide 99% of personnel in the International Security Assistance Force (ISAF) in Afghanistan.[1] In the first ten months of 2002, the EU pledged € 60 million in aid to Afghanistan, of two-thirds of which had been allotted by October. However, EU members did not use ESDP to rally their military resources, even though conflict management is a core function of ESDP.

The renewed interest in crisis management and reconstruction highlights the international need for skills the EU has been developing. EU initiatives address both conflict prevention and management. In the wake of genocide in Rwanda, carnage in Bosnia, and other crises of the 1990s, many analysts and policymakers sought to improve international capacities for conflict prevention. The argument went that not only did the international community need to be able to contain or stop mass violence; it should try to avert the recourse to violence in the first place. Not surprisingly countries such as Sweden with a tradition of peacekeeping and humanitarian activity were active in this effort. Once it acceded to the EU in 1995, Sweden became an ardent advocate of enhancing the EU's role in conflict prevention, especially during its 2001 Presidency of the European Union.

Many observers have developed frameworks for analyzing conflict prevention capacities. One prominent analysis divides conflict prevention into "operational" and "structural" prevention.[2] Operational prevention entails actions to forestall imminent conflict. These include early warning and response, preventive diplomacy, economic sanctions and inducements, and the use of force. Structural prevention addresses the longer-term causes of conflict. These include security, economic and social well-being, and justice. The EU is developing capacities for both types of prevention.

EU Policies, ESDP, and International Peacekeeping

The Petersberg tasks lie at the core of the EU's approach to conflict prevention. Incorporating the Western European Union's 1992 statement, the EU's 1997 Amsterdam Treaty lists them as "humanitarian and rescue tasks, peacekeeping tasks, and tasks of combat forces in crisis management, including peacemaking." What makes the EU a potentially significant contributor to international security is the ability to combine civilian and military resources to manage violent conflicts.

The EU presents itself as able to combine traditional "hard" military power with nontraditional "soft" power. The latter includes diplomatic support, political influence, economic inducements, development assistance and other nonmilitary tools. The EU brings together fifteen countries that already have diplomatic clout and major economic power. If European leaders want to exert soft power, they do not have to create it. Instead they have to construct the mechanisms to pool and channel the soft power that they already have. In effect, the EU is mixing hard and soft power as it builds capacities in civilian crisis management. Developing capacities for operational prevention and for peacemaking and peacekeeping after a conflict is a new activity for the EU and commands much of the political attention, because they concern one of the hallmarks of state power—the use of force. ESDP is particularly relevant for two aspects of operational prevention: early warning and the use of force. Two other aspects of operational prevention, preventive diplomacy and economic measures, are instruments of a Common Foreign and Security Policy, of which ESDP is a separate component.

Early warning and response is the first element of conflict management, because it identifies the types of crises an institution intends to address. For example, if a country only considers threats from other states, it will not track internal conditions. The EU approach does consider internal conditions. In accordance with the EU program on the Prevention of Violent Conflicts, the European Commission maintains a "checklist for root causes of conflict/early warning indicators."[3] At the beginning of each six-month EU Presidency the Commission and the Secretary-General/High Representative for CFSP evaluate over 120 countries and prepare a "watch list" for the General Affairs and Externals Relations Council. The checklist outlines eight areas for review:

1. Legitimacy of the State

2. Rule of Law

3. Respect for Fundamental Rights

4. Civil society and media

5. Relations between communities and dispute-solving mechanisms

6. Sound economic management

7. Social and regional inequalities

8. Geopolitical situation

Thus, the EU is beginning to develop its own mechanisms for conflict analysis. Conflict prevention could necessitate combining civilian and military assets and, hence, planning that includes both types of resources. Although national governments have both kinds of capacities, most international organizations do not. The most powerful alliance, the North Atlantic Treaty Organization, is a military organization and does not have access to the full-range of civilian tools the EU hopes to use. In its analysis of the role of civilian tools in conflict management, the EU will have to rely on its own procedures, as NATO's approach is less relevant.[4] EU member states may also share some of the result their own extensive analysis conducted by foreign or defense ministries. Intelligence sharing plays a role in early warning as well as the conduct of operations but is one of the most politically sensitive aspects of ESDP. Moreover, early warning only matters if it leads to an effective response. ESDP can enhance the EU's analysis of conflicts, but the High Representative for CFSP and national governments are needed to summon the political will to act.

Much of the work on ESDP focuses on the difficult challenge of constructing a mechanism for the EU to exert military force. The use of force by the EU for conflict management raises several difficult questions of EU member states. Firstly, there is a building tension between the developing ESDP as a mechanism for managing "low-end," low intensity conflict similar to traditional UN peacekeeping, and creating a high-tech, "high-end" facility able to deploy to violent situations and able to engage in operations with the most advanced U.S. forces. The Headline Goals outline military and civilian capacities. The Rapid Reaction Facility would enable the EU to deploy forces to a conflict to prevent the outbreak or the spread of violence. Secondly, there is a latent disagreement about who can authorize the use of force. All EU member states would prefer that EU military assets would be deployed on authorization of the United Nations or the Organization for Security and Cooperation in Europe (OSCE). What if neither were available? Would European military assets then not be available through the EU? The fact that the EU is a group of states, and the exigencies of UN or OSCE authorization, mean that military assets organized under the auspices of the EU would probably only be deployed in situations where there were widespread international agreement on the need for military action by outsiders.

According to the Petersberg tasks, ESDP could be used for peacekeeping or peacemaking. Several analysts have stressed that effective peacekeeping operations need a lead country to serve as the catalyst and organizer of the international response.[5] Given the capacities of its constituent states the EU could be candidate to be a lead "state." Several of its member countries have served as a lead state. Does ESDP enhance the EU's ability to be a lead state? Len Hawley outlines ten "Key Attributes of a Capable Lead Nation:"[6]

- Recognized disposition for non-intervention in the region
- Strong domestic support for long, hard, costly commitments
- High-level personal diplomacy by political and military leadership
- Effective diplomatic connections to supporting major power
- Previous defense cooperation arrangements in the region
- Professional competencies of the nation's defense forces
- Internal intelligence collection capacity—both political and security
- Strong financial management capacity for the coalition
- Sophisticated public information and media affairs capacity
- A well-founded international reputation

The EU has or could develop some of the characteristics of a lead "state." Collective action under an EU flag could provide the cloak of a disposition towards non-intervention. This could help the EU be acceptable in regions where a member state is a former colonial power. Conversely, the EU could be used to mask, but still serve, particular national policy. EU officials are farther away from citizens, so could have a harder time building the case for costly commitments, but respected leaders such as Solana and Patten can provide high-level personal diplomacy. The creation of a High Representative for CFSP enhances the EU's role in this area. EU member states are the connections to a supporting major power(s). Member states may have previous defense arrangements that they could offer to an EU-led operation, and they provide the core professional competencies and intelligence capability. The general secretariat of the Council of the EU that administers ESDP facilitates use of the defense arrangements, professional capacities and intelligence assets. The Headline Goals are part of this process. Cooperative mechanisms within the EU can help ensure strong financial management and sophisticated media affairs. However with reference to Hawley's last point, the EU is still building its international reputation in the security area. On balance, the administrative mechanisms of ESDP could improve Europeans' ability to work together to play the role of a "lead" nation in peace operations. ESDP could improve their capacity to act, but national leaders still need to be vocal advocates of the need to act.

Another way in which ESDP could contribute to international security is to bolster the mechanisms for United Nations peacekeeping. The 2000 Report of the Panel on United Nations Peace Operations, known as the "Brahimi Report" after the panel's chairman, outlined several ways to improve United Nations peacekeeping capacities. If ESDP is to contribute to UN peacekeeping, does it accord with the themes of the Brahimi report? Among a variety of recommendations, the Brahimi Report calls for member states to take several steps including improving the UN Stand-by arrangements system (UNSAS), and developing stand-by lists of "civilian police, international judicial experts, penal experts, and human rights specialists."[7] The Headline Goals for the rule of law create such lists. Thus, ESDP could facilitate the EU's work with the UN Department of Peacekeeping Operations on catalogue of capacities in the area of the rule of law.

The inclusion of the civilian aspects is one of the most important contributions ESDP could make to conflict prevention capacities beyond simply an agglomeration of national military assets. At the June 2000 Feira meeting, the European Council adopted four priority areas for civilian Headline Goals: police, rule of law, civilian administration, and civil protection. The notion is to build up the capability to field teams that can provide comprehensive and integrated security support, especially in the aftermath of conflict when local people are trying to rebuild their community. In these situations, outsiders can help by maintaining law and order, while local institutions are rebuilt. The EU Headline Goal recognizes that civilian police need to be complemented by support for the judicial system.

The EU is committed to developing both types of international civilian police capacity: those that train local police and those that provide security directly. At the November 2001 Police Capabilities Commitment Conference, national governments made pledges that would enable the EU to meet its target of hiving 5,000 police officers available by 2003 (with 1,000 being deployable within 30 days). This is an increase over the approximately 3,500 European police officers currently serving in international operations.

At its June 2001 Göteborg meeting, the European Council also set targets for the other aspects of civilian conflict management, which were further expanded at the June 2002 European Council meeting. EU member states offered pledges at the May 16, 2002 Rule of Law Capabilities Conference. The table summarizes the goals.[8]

Area	Target
Civilian Police	5,000 available by 2003 (1,000 within 30 days)
Rule of Law	Goal was 200 judges, prosecutors, and other criminal justice professionals; 282 have been pledged with 60 available in 30 days. (Includes 72 judges, 48 prosecutors, 38 administrative services, 72 penitentiary officials, 34 others)
Civil Administration	Pool of experts who could take on administrative jobs at short notice (no specific number set)
Civil Protection	Teams of up to 2,000 people that could intervene on short notice; member states would provide assessment and other specialized resources

The June 2002 "Presidency Report on European Security and Defense Policy" urges member states to improve their ability to deploy prosecutors and other officials to "ensure a complete and functioning criminal justice process in operations in which international police perform an executive role." Thus, when the EU police are enforcing laws directly, EU member states should have the capacity to send judicial officials to support the system as a whole. The Council Secretariat gathers the data in the Coordinating Mechanism for Civilian Aspects of Crisis Management. Also, the rule of law experts are available for fact-finding missions, giving the EU another diplomatic tool.

Perhaps one of the most innovative developments could be the EU's work on "civil protection." One component of civil protection is the national governments' mechanisms to respond to "natural, technological, and environmental emergencies" in EU member states and other countries.[9] However, the notion of civil protection goes beyond national arrangements to include a Community Mechanism for reinforced cooperation in civil protection interventions. The report of the 2001 Göteborg European Council describes the specific targets set for civil protection:[10]

- 2-3 assessment and/or co-ordination teams consisting in all of 10 experts, that could be dispatched within 3—7 hours, depending on the circumstances. The experts should be on 24 hour call from a group of up to 100 specially selected experts for this purpose;

- Civil Protection intervention teams consisting of up to 2,000 persons at very short notice;

- supplementary or more specialised resources from the competent services or, where relevant, non-governmental organisations and other entities in response to the specific needs in each crisis, that could be dispatched within 2 days to a week.

The notion of civil protection could provide scope for fast action by the EU in a crisis in Europe or beyond if leaders chose to use it. In a crisis, the rotating presidency of the Council of the European Union could initiate action. After consultations with the Council and the Commission, the Presidency "may request civil protection assistance" from national assets provided through the Community Mechanism. Thus, an activist EU Presidency could highlight the need for civil protection in a crisis situation. As noted in the Göteborg European Council report, civil protection has been called upon in complex crises to help with humanitarian relief ". . . covering the immediate survival and protection needs of affected population . . . search and rescue, [and] construction of refuges camps . . ."[11] In an October 23, 2001 decision, the European Council agreed to create the Community Mechanism (which went into force on January 1, 2002), and confirmed that "such a Community Mechanisms could, under conditions to be determined, also be a tool for facilitating and supporting crisis management . . ."[12] Military forces may be contributed to civil protection. Also there could be opportunities for the accession countries and non-EU members to participate in the Community Mechanism. Therefore, a wide range of EU assets could be deployed in a crisis under the rubric of civil protection.

The combination of civilian police and other post-conflict judicial and administrative expertise gives the EU important assets to help war-torn societies rebuild. Too often the international community commits resources in the immediate aftermath of war, but cannot sustain its engagement. Bringing together the right resources to deal with complex emergencies requires crossing bureaucratic lines to gain contributions from aid agencies, foreign, defense, and—in the case of many police forces—interior ministries. In addition, government authorities may have to work with nongovernmental organizations providing relief.

While ESDP has the potential to expand European conflict prevention and management capabilities, ESDP is also bound by important constraints. Member states disagree on their hypotheses about where ESDP could be used. In effect, ESDP is limited in geographic scope. Some European leaders think ESDP could be used in regions near Europe such as North Africa or the Middle East. Other leaders act as if ESDP should be used no farther than the Balkans. The EU's lack of strategic lift reinforces the implicit regional focus, at least for the short term. Even if geographically limited the EU's combination of political, economic, and military tools could be helpful. In the context of CFSP, the EU is already playing a more assertive role in the Arab-Israeli conflict, with the EU a member of the diplomatic Quartet along with the United States, the Russian Federation, and the United Nations.

Some of the most critical demands for a lead nation to rally international support to prevent or mitigate conflict are likely to occur outside Europe. If there were renewed violence in parts of sub-Saharan Africa, would the EU use the resources of ESDP to contain the violence as the United Kingdom did in Sierra Leone or France did in Rwanda? EU forces would need airlift to get to the region in question. Moreover, consideration of EU military activity in member states' traditional areas of influence could raise concerns, especially in the United Kingdom and France, which still retain broad international interests.

ESDP is also constrained by member states' different views of what the Petersberg tasks really entail. Countries, such as Sweden, which retains neutrality and has a long history of UN peacekeeping, tend to emphasize ESDP's contribution to preventive action and peace operations. Conversely, the United Kingdom and France highlighted "the capacity for autonomous action, backed up by credible military forces" in the 1998 St Malo statement.[13] After the war in Afghanistan some policy analysts began to argue that Europeans should focus on developing technical capacities in a few specialized areas to a high standard in order to be able to fight in coalition with the United States. In September 2002 meeting of NATO defense ministers, U.S. Secretary of Defense Donald Rumsfeld floated the idea of a high-end NATO Response Force. This "spearhead" approach could create very different requirements for European resources than does ESDP. Careful leadership will be needed to make ESDP and NATO's Response Force complementary rather than competitive.

If ESDP does not progress, it would be a set back not only for the EU, but for international peacekeeping. The EU could make ESDP capacities and organization available for international peacekeeping. This is clearly one of the Petersberg tasks. What is not clear is whether European leaders—and their publics—consider ESDP peacekeeping to be limited the Balkans or other regions in or near Europe or whether ESDP can be used in service of United Nations peacekeeping farther afield.

Real events are the test of ESDP's capacities for conflict prevention and management. In the aftermath of the September 11 terrorist attacks, the EU took important steps to implement financial constraints on terrorists and improve cooperation on justice and home affairs. However, EU member states offered military assets bilaterally rather than through the EU. Furthermore, Germany may take the lead on ISAF in Afghanistan, but it will draw on the resources of NATO to do so, not ESDP. The EU faces another test when it takes over executive police functions in Bosnia and Herzegovina on January 1, 2003, following the United Nations operation. The EU takes up this job with the agreement of the government of Bosnia and Herzegovina and the support of the UN Security Council (Resolution 1396).

Yet the European Union is not the first economic organization to deploy military force. The Economic Community of West African States (ECOWAS) was the institution its member states used to mount a peacekeeping operation in Liberia and later in Sierra Leone. Countries in the area realized that western states were not going to support a United Nations operation, so the ECOWAS members marshaled their own effort, the ECOWAS Monitoring Group (ECOMOG). Like EU members facing the Balkans, ECOWAS members were spurred to action by a hemorrhaging crisis in their neighborhood. Regional hegemon Nigeria was the driving force behind the deployment of ECOMOG. Interestingly, in a region long protective of state sovereignty, ECOMOG was already in Liberia before it received a UN mandate. The crisis was considered so severe that constraining the violence offered its own legitimacy. Like EU members, ECOWAS members wanted UN sanction, but they were willing to act first as support from the Security Council's permanent members was not initially forthcoming. Moreover, like the EU, ECOWAS had to accommodate the contrasting styles of its members. Whereas Nigeria practiced a robust form of peacemaking, Ghana was a leader in a more consensual form of peacekeeping. New scholarship is beginning to explore the lessons of ECOMOG for other regional organizations.[14] The EU could look to ECOWAS for lessons on using an organization that was initially economic to field a military force.

U.S. and EU views of international conflict

Under the Bush Administration, the United States and the European Union take different views of the nature of conflict, especially in light of the anti-terrorism campaign. The anti-terrorism campaign shapes the Administration's analyses of conflict. The chapters in the concluding section of the book treat divergent U.S. and European attitudes in greater detail. At this point we can note that both the EU and the U.S. stress the need for early engagement in crises, but while the EU Petersberg tasks stress conflict prevention and peacekeeping, the United States under the Bush Administration asserts a right of preemptive military action. In contrast, the EU notes that prevention is an obligation of UN member states.[15]

Only time will tell whether managing non-traditional conflicts will link or divide the transatlantic community. Many European countries already have a long history of peacekeeping. A version of ESDP that enables the EU to play a greater role in peace operations could enhance the standing of Europeans' strategic contributions among Washington policymakers, especially among those who have long called for greater burden-sharing. Improved EU-wide mechanisms for contributing to peacekeeping can be supported both by Americans who value peacekeeping and by Americans who want to release U.S. forces for other operations. If the evolving EU capacities can also bolster UN peacekeeping, then the rest of the international community might cheer for it too.

Notes:

1. In August 2002, Europeans accounted for 4,973 of the people out of a total of 4,998. New Zealand provided six, and the United States nineteen. See list of ISAF contributors and approximate personnel levels at "European Defense" available at www.european-defense.co.uk.

2. Carnegie Commission on Preventing Deadly Conflict, *Preventing Deadly Conflict Final Report* (Washington, D.C.: Carnegie Commission on Preventing Deadly Conflict, 1997).

3. European Commission, "European Commission Check-list for Root Causes of Conflict," http://www.europa.eu.int/comm/external_relations/ cpcm/cp/list.htm, accessed September 3, 2002.

4. Carlo Jean, *An Integrated Civil Police Force for the European Union.* (Brussels: Centre for European Policy Studies, 2002).

5. Carnegie Commission on Preventing Deadly Conflict, *Preventing Deadly Conflict Final Report*, p. 40, and Mr. Len Hawley, former United States Deputy Assistant Secretary of State for International Organization Affairs.

6. Len Hawley, "Achieving Success in U.S. Policy with a Complex Contingency Operation," unpublished paper, 2002.

7. United Nations General Assembly and Security Council, *Report of the Panel on United Nations Peace Operations.* A/55/305 and S/2000/809. Full report available at www.un.org. Summary of recommendations available at www.un.org/peace/reports/peace_operations/docs/recommend.htm.

8. Göteborg European Council, Presidency Conclusions, Annex III, available at http://ue.eu.int/newsroom/newmain.asp?lang=1 and Council of the European Union, "Rule of Law Capabilities Commitment Conference Declaration," Annex I of the "Presidency Report on European Security and Defense Policy," Brussels, June 22, 2002.

9. Presidency Report to the Göteborg European Council on European Security and Defense Policy, Annex III "New concrete targets for civilian aspects of crisis management," paragraph 42, available at http://ue.eu.int/Newsroom/LoadDoc.asp?BID=75&DID=66829&LAN G=1.

10. Presidency Report to the Göteborg European Council on European Security and Defense Policy, Annex III "New concrete targets for civilian aspects of crisis management," paragraph 47.

11. Ibid, para. 44.

12. Presidency Report on European Security and Defense Policy, following the General Affairs Council of January 17, 2002 (Brussels, June 22, 2002), 10160/2/02 REV 2, Annex III, "The Use in Crisis Management, Referred to in Title V of the Treaty of the European Union, of the Community Mechanisms to Facilitate the Reinforced Cooperation in Civil Protection Assistance Interventions," paragraph 3.

13. British-French Summit, Joint Declaration, St. Malo, December 3-4, 1998, para.2.

14. See the forthcoming paper by Funmi Olonisakin, for the International Peace Academy.

15. Partners in Prevention, Regional EU Conference on Conflict Prevention, August 2002.

ESDP and Transatlantic Relations

ESDP and Global Security Challenges: Will There Be a "Division of Labor" Between Europe and the United States?

Bruno Tertrais

Old ideas, new realities

The question of a possible "division of labor" between Allies on defense and security has been debated for decades, linked as it was to the poisonous issue of "sharing the security burden" between Americans and Europeans. As a U.S. analyst puts it, *"tensions relating to burden-sharing have been the snake in the garden of NATO since its inception."*[1] The return of U.S. forces to Europe after the Second World War was seen by Washington as a temporary measure,[2] and the United States urged its European partners to provide more troops for the defense of the continent. In April 1951, the U.S. Senate voted resolution 99 which called for the Europeans to make the major contribution to allied ground troops.[3]

The resilience of this debate stems of course from the fundamental asymmetry in NATO. A maritime power located an ocean away, the United States has sought to rely mostly on air power and naval forces, as well as on nuclear weapons, to fulfill its Alliance commitments. It was only natural in American eyes that the Europeans, which had more manpower-intensive forces and were defending their own countries, would provide the bulk of territorial defense. As a result, the debate on burden-sharing often reflected, in the eyes of the Europeans, the U.S. desire for a form of division of labor in which Washington provided the high-tech means and Europe provided the land forces—thus implying a "division of risks" which in their minds was breaking the Alliance's conceptual backbone, the "sharing of risks and responsibilities."

Subsequently, Europe's growing international role has allowed Washington's allies to point out that they were taking a much bigger share than the United States of non-military assistance to countries in transition and developing nations, and increasingly so. Arguing that the post-Cold War realities allow for a broader definition of "security," they were trying to demonstrate that the burden was much more evenly distributed than what the U.S. critics of Europe were willing to admit. Today, the European Union and its member states provide more than 50% of international development aid and humanitarian aid ($ 25.4 billion compared to $ 9.6 billion for the United States).[4] The same disparity exists in terms of United Nations (UN) funding.[5] Furthermore, European states will bear the main responsibility for financing the reduction in the U.S. contribution to the UN following the December 2000 agreement, at a total cost of about $ 150 million a year. (All in all, the European Union will provide for almost *half* of the UN total costs by 2003.) Also, Europe has taken on the main burden of state and nation-building in the Balkans: in 2000 Europe had spent, on average, three times more than the United States for non-military assistance in the Balkans (nearly $ 17 billion against $ 5.5 billion);[6] and the European Union bears between 75 and 80% of all reconstruction, assistance and administration costs in Kosovo.

To be sure, Congressional and other critics of Europe in the United States are only mildly interested in hearing about the EU's development funds and contributions to the United Nations. What they are interested in is saving dollars from the U.S. defense budget. To which the Europeans answer that they provide host nation support for the presence of U.S. troops in Europe; that they provide the bulk of NATO's Reaction Forces,[7] etc. Thus, the division of labor debate has been, to a large extent, a dialogue of the deaf.

In recent years, three factors have shed a new light on this debate.

First, the EU member States have committed themselves to the development of a European Security and Defense Policy (ESDP), that is an autonomous capacity to take decisions and organize crisis management operations backed up by credible military forces.[8] Operation *Allied Force* boosted the concept of an ESDP by revealing the limitations of European military power. At the same time, the war in Kosovo also showed the limits of NATO as an instrument of collective crisis management, and in this regard had an additional impact on the drive for an ESDP. To many Europeans, *Allied Force* revealed an authoritarian attitude of Washington towards Alliance decision-making, and a U.S. tendency to bypass NATO altogether by using its own national chain of command. At the same time, for the Americans, it revealed the inadequacies of consensus at 19 as a *modus operandi* for high-intensity crisis management. As former U.S. ambassador to NATO Robert Hunter said, Kosovo was probably *"the farthest bridge"* for the Alliance.[9] Therefore, although triggered by an event resorting to Article 5 (and which caused many European casualties), operation *Enduring Freedom* was planned and organized entirely by the United States. But, in turn, some in Europe have interpreted that move as the demise of NATO as a military instrument, reinforcing their belief in the need for a strong ESDP.[10]

Therefore, with ESDP, Europe wants to become an actor capable of taking charge on its own of significant military missions, with better-organized and better-equipped forces. That could make it possible to imagine new concepts of division of labor as well as burden-sharing.

Second, post-Cold War crisis management operations have confirmed the longstanding tendency for Americans to provide the bulk of high-tech means while Europeans provide forces on the ground. On average, during the 1990s Europe provided 75% of all ground troops in the Balkans. In 1996, the "peak" year of U.S. ground deployments, forces provided by Washington represented only 31%, and in 2001, European nations provided about 72% of all NATO forces in the region (43,000 vs. 11,000 for the U.S.). At the same time, the transatlantic gap on high-technology capabilities has become, if not more pronounced, at least certainly most visible and embarrassing for the Europeans, since assets for which there is a clear discrepancy between allies are increasingly recognized as being indispensable for crisis management. That is true in particular of all-weather precision bombing. During the Gulf war, U.S. forces provided for 85% of all air sorties and nearly 90% of precision munitions. Eight years later, during the Kosovo war—a NATO operation in Europe—the proportions were barely different: U.S. forces accounted for 70-80% of all strike sorties and about 80% of precision munitions. According to one estimate, out of 5,000 military aircraft available in European armed forces, barely 10% are capable of precision bombing.[11]

Third, the policy preferences of the Bush administration, which have been considerably strengthened by the war on terrorism, have given birth to the concept of "backfilling," whereby the Europeans would have the prime responsibility for low-intensity missions and operations, notably in the Balkans, ensuring the free availability of U.S. military forces for high-intensity combat missions, and more generally for the management of "hard security" issues, in particular in the Middle East and Asia.[12] As early as October 2001, the United States had begun redeploying some ships from the Mediterranean that were replaced by European ones.

The question then becomes whether or not these two latter trends will develop into a more formal "division of labor" acknowledged, accepted and encouraged by both sides.

Conceptual approaches and reality check

Let us therefore examine the credibility of several possible concepts for a transatlantic division of labor on defense and security.

From a conceptual point of view, there are four models for the security relationship between the United States and Europe: competing in the "market" of security responsibilities and power play; working together within a single institutional framework, as they do today in NATO; establishing a hierarchy between NATO and the European Union, with the former taking precedence over the latter in a form of "subsidiarity";[13] and dividing responsibilities between the United States and the European Union, or NATO and the European Union, which is the "division of labor" model *per se*.

We begin with concepts for a "geographical" division of labor.

The area of responsibility is one criterion to define a possible division of labor between NATO and the European Union. NATO operates only in Europe—not that there would be anything in the Treaty that legally precludes the organization to do otherwise, but most Alliance members have consistently resisted the idea of operating "out-of-area" or embracing the concept of a "global NATO." Despite the participation of most Alliance members, NATO was not used to conduct operation *Desert Storm*. To be sure, since the end of the Cold war NATO has moved well beyond the Article 5 area by embarking in peace support operations in the Balkans. But the 1999 Strategic Concept made clear that NATO's area of interest was the "Euro-Atlantic" region, and the organization does not have military commands responsible for operations outside that region. After 9/11, NATO planes operated outside Europe (over the territory of the United States) for the first time; but this was a limited mission remaining within the boundaries of the Article 5 region. The military organization as such was not used to wage the war on terrorism, be it in Afghanistan or elsewhere. By contrast, the geographical scope of action of the European Union is theoretically unlimited. In 1987 and 1990-1991, the Western European Union (WEU) operated in the Gulf whereas NATO was not. So, in principle at least, there could be a division of labor by which NATO acts in Europe, and the European Union acts elsewhere.

However, such a division of labor does not reflect current trends.

First, the European Union too intends to be able to operate on the continent. Despite initial U.S. wishes, the "subsidiarity" model has been discarded when defining the relationship between the two organizations. The Europeans did not want to give NATO a "right of first refusal," and argued in particular to that effect that, in any case, the process of informal consultations that accompanies any crisis management would render meaningless the institution of any formal mechanism. Hence the now-agreed formula in official texts according to which the European Union might act "*where* NATO as a whole is not engaged" (as opposed to "*when*," despite the occasional slip-of-the-tongue by U.S. officials).[14]

Second, another effect of the war on terrorism has been to start a trend by which the European Union might replace NATO in maintaining the peace in the Balkans. That is what is being done in Macedonia.

Third, the NATO allies have begun exploring ways through which the Alliance could be made more effective in dealing with unexpected high-intensity crises away from Europe (such as counter-terriorism Article 5 operations): this is the rationale for the creation of a small non permanent "NATO Response Force."

Another way to conceive a geographical transatlantic division of labor would be one where the Europeans have the prime responsibility to maintain the peace in Europe, while the United States would manage global security challenges, in particular in the Middle East and in Asia. The European Union's projection means to this day remain limited; in particular, it lacks autonomous strategic airlift capabilities. At the same time, it is fair to argue that "*European defense begins at home.*"[15] Geography impacts the definition of security interests. The Union cannot afford to disregard the Balkans: if Washington were to withdraw from all NATO operations, it would have to replace U.S. forces: *"whatever the cost, Europe would have to stay. For Europe, there can be no 'exit strategy' from the Balkans."*[16] Another reason is that the United States has defense commitments in East Asia that Europe does not have. (Already during the Viet-Nam war, the U.S. Administration wanted increased European commitment for the defense of the continent in order to free some forces for engagement in Asia.)[17] Also, the Washington is increasingly concerned by the rise of China and the possible challenges it raises for Asian security, an issue Europeans do not seem very interested in.[18]

However, this idea runs contrary to both parties' policies.

First, both want the United States to continue to be engaged in European security and in common military operations. This is true first for the European side. It is useful to remind that developing an ESDP was never about throwing America out of Europe: for some, it was in fact quite the opposite—that is, a way to *secure* the continuation of the U.S. engagement on the continent by answering Washington's call for a better burden-sharing. That was already one of the rationales put forward for a European Defense Community in the early 1950s. President Bush and Chancellor Schröder made a clear joint statement to that effect in March 2001, welcoming ESDP *"as an important contribution to sharing the burden of security and peace which will strengthen the Atlantic Alliance."*[19] Most Europeans welcome the continuation of the U.S. role as a peacekeeper and balancer in Europe, a sentiment going way beyond the Atlantic Alliance: Central and Eastern European nations, NATO aspirants and Balkan war parties alike, consider that a strong U.S. military presence on the continent provides them with a unique political and security guarantee.[20] In particular, the security situation in Eastern Europe has not evolved to the point where one could say that Article 5 on the continent is now irrelevant. Europeans also acknowledge—even if sometimes to regret it—that the United States plays also a useful role to defuse crises between its allies, like it did for instance, to take recent examples, in 1995 during the Greece-Turkey crisis, and in 2002 during the Spain-Morocco tensions. (Critics of the European Union's inability to solve such crises on its own miss the point: it is hardly up to an organization to mediate between one of its members and another state.)

This is true also for the U.S. side. The United States has political, economic and security interests in Europe that warrants the continuation of a significant military involvement on the continent. And the weight of national or ethnic groups of European origin (Greek, Irish, Lithuanian, Polish, etc.) in U.S. political decision-making ensures that U.S. administrations will be inclined to maintain a strong role in managing key European issues.[21] It is true that many Republicans have long urged the Europeans to take charge of the peacekeeping tasks in the Balkans now that most of fighting is over. During the presidential campaign, Dick Cheney made it clear that in such circumstances it was "*appropriate*" for European ground troops to take over.[22] Condoleezza Rice confirmed this view: the National Security Adviser-to-be bluntly said in October 2000 that extended peacekeeping "*detracts from our readiness*" for missions such as the protection of Saudi Arabia and Taiwan;[23] according to her it was not the U.S. military's job to "escort children to the Kindergarten." Here again we encounter echoes of a recurrent theme in the transatlantic security debate: the Europeans traditionally suspect the United States to be willing to take the responsibilities without taking the risks, and to rely mostly on air and sea power rather than on the stationing of exposed ground forces. But the concept of "in together, out together" remains the Alliance's motto. It has been the case since the Dayton agreements, with a view to avoid a return to the years 1991-1995 when the United States and Europe disagreed on policies and strategies to manage the Yugoslav wars (and more broadly to avoid making NATO irrelevant). "Togetherness" and American presence on the ground have been adopted by the Bush administration and thus continue to be U.S. official policy. Opposed by some of the most "hawkish" officials in Washington, this policy nevertheless remains widely supported in the U.S. security community (including, it seems, the U.S. Army itself).[24]

Second, both parties are interested in the Europeans having a security role outside their continent. The United States wants to have the Europeans participating in Middle East and Asian wars (arguably on their own terms). Despite the publicity given to the "divergence of interests" thesis, most analysts in the U.S. security studies community traditionally favor a "partnership" model between the United States and Europe rather than a "division of labor" model.[25] This is also true of the U.S. public opinion.[26] And while several EU members—not only the "neutrals" or "non-aligned," but also some NATO members—do not want ESDP to be a vehicle for military adventurism all over the world, most member States agree that the Union has global interests warranting concrete security actions in such regions. This is already true in the Middle East. The European Union is the main provider of non-military assistance in the region, in particular for the Palestinian territories, and would certainly be ready to send troops to implement or monitor a future peace plan. Europe is also interested in security in the Gulf, from which an important share of its oil supplies comes; its first ever common military actions took place in that region in 1987, for the protection of oil shipments. And France and the United Kingdom, which were important partners in operation *Desert Storm*, have U.S.-like defense commitments towards several Gulf countries. Thus Europe will not want to "leave" the management of Middle East security to the United States. Not as much can be said about Asia; but the European Union has also begun to be active in that region, with concrete actions ranging today from humanitarian actions in East Timor to common policy actions such as the EU visit to North Korea, or the training of local police forces as discussed at the latest ASEM (ASia-Europe Meeting).

Alternatively, one could imagine that the European Union would devise its own version of the Monroe doctrine and would consider, neo-colonialist connotations aside, that for geographical and historical reasons Africa is its strategic "backyard" like Latin America is traditionally considered a U.S. "backyard." But, again, commercial and political interests of both parties render today such a division of labor unrealistic. Also, the Europeans resent what they see as a U.S. tendency to discharge themselves of some global responsibilities on their allies. During the Clinton era, the hard-line view according to which "the U.S. should not do windows" was not official policy. But things seem to have changed. In addition to the aforementioned comments by Condoleezza Rice, many in Europe were dismayed by the convergence of views between vice-President Gore and Governor Bush in the run-up to the 2000 U.S. election, when the two then-presidential hopefuls candidly said in a nationwide televised debate that intervening in humanitarian disasters such as Rwanda was not a U.S. responsibility because no "vital" U.S. interest was involved. Again, strategic and commercial interests dictate that the Europeans might be more prompt to intervene in Africa than the United States; but the Europeans would also expect that a tragedy of such magnitude as that of Rwanda would transcend immediate interests and be considered by all Western allies as a cause deserving common action.

Finally, to discard the geographic approach once and for all, let us suggest that any geographical division of labor implies renouncing a synergy of efforts between the U.S. and Europe, each with its own assets and capabilities; in other words, what economic theory says is the optimum solution for the production of goods does not make sense for the management of security.

We now turn to the concept of a "functional" division of labor.

A possibility would be that Alliance members consider that NATO is responsible for combat operations, and the European Union for humanitarian, peace support and civilian tasks (such as police missions, reconstruction, and "nation-building" in general). Such a division of labor could also broadly apply to the United States and the European Union. It is true that *"the EU has some unique advantages in dealing with situations in a holistic way—including political, civilian, nongovernmental organization, and economic instruments—that NATO cannot match,"* and thus offers, as argued elsewhere in this volume, "one-stop shopping" for security management.[27] And the Worldviews study shows that Europeans are much more willing than Americans to use force in order to end a civil war.[28]

However, the Europeans are not interested in limiting themselves to such tasks.

First, the European Union's defense policy concept, reflecting its political ambitions, is much broader than just humanitarian and traditional, "blue-helmet" type peacekeeping. When seeking to reassure Washington, some allies downplay this fact.[29] It is true that so far, EU military planning remains prudent and focuses mostly on humanitarian and peacekeeping operations in and around the continent. However, the so-called "Petersberg tasks" explicitly include combat missions and peacemaking, and cover "everything but collective defense."[30] This does not necessarily mean that the EU seeks to be able to do an *Allied Force*-type operation on its own. (In fact, faced alone with a Kosovo-type situation, the European Union would probably have tried to manage it otherwise; which is not to say that it would have succeeded.) And, again, some EU members show great cautiousness in this domain: Nordic countries, for instance, have little appetite for EU high-intensity combat operations.[31] Still, the intent of the Petersberg drafters was clear as to the inclusion of "hard" security missions.[32] While France is probably the most vocal opponent of a "hard security/soft security" division of labor, there is generally speaking a growing convergence of views in Europe according to which the Union should be a full-fledged military power.[33] Interestingly, the Worldviews study shows that a large majority of Europeans are as willing to use force as Americans.[34] The transatlantic debate of 1990 to 1995 has been described as opposing Washington, willing to use force, and the Europeans, afraid that it would endanger their peace-keeping effort on the ground: in fact, no government in the Alliance was willing to enforce peace in the Balkans until 1995.[35]

Using force could include combat operations on the continent itself. Most European leaders are aware that ensuring peace at the fringes of the continent will not necessarily be a tea party. With the coming enlargement, the European Union is bound to encounter *"the Hobbesian realities of life."*[36] The war against terrorism has also prompted a debate on the need for the European Union to build a "spearhead" force, or a common special operations unit. Finally, while there is a consensus in the Union that NATO remains the natural vehicle for mutual defense against aggression (the Washington treaty's Article 5) on the continent, the future EU agenda could go beyond the Petersberg tasks, and one day include collective defense. During the 1990s, some in France and Germany have called for the insertion of the Brussels treaty's own Article 5 into the Treaty on the European Union, and nowadays Paris is trying to convince its partners to include a mutual security assistance clause in EU texts. (The treaty itself mentions safeguarding the *"integrity"* of the Union as an objective of CFSP, and explicitly includes the possibility of a *"common defense, should the European Council so decide."*)

Second, during combined operations in the pursuit of common goals, be it stability on the Old Continent or the reduction of the terrorist threat, the Europeans are not keen to leave the sole responsibility of high-intensity combat missions to the United States. In this respect, they often resent what they call a U.S. tendency to leave them the "dirty work" of keeping the peace and financing reconstruction.[37] "The Americans do the cooking and we wash the dishes," said some

Europeans during the Afghan campaign (to which one might add that they also defined the recipe and the seating plan on their own, given that the allied input in strategic and operational planning in operation *Enduring Freedom* was almost non-existent). Granted, European armed forces today are deficient in many key capabilities needed for high-intensity crisis management, such all-weather precision strike, strategic lift, as well as command, control, communications and intelligence (C3I). But they plan to remedy to these deficiencies.

The United States consistently encourages them to do so since it would benefit to the Alliance as a whole. One should note, in this respect, that *only an ambitious ESDP carries indirect benefits for Washington*: that of better-armed and better-trained allies.[38] What is good for the EU is also good for NATO. U.S. analyst Kori Shake rightly emphasizes that the European Union would *"gain America's respect by focusing on improvements at the war-fighting end of the Petersberg tasks."*[39] And as French then-defense minister Alain Richard subtly remarked in 2001, *"Our American allies must be able to decide on their participation in the management of a crisis without being constrained by European impotence to endorse alone the choice between action and abstention."*[40] On the contrary, a division of labor where the United States does high-altitude bombing and the allies does the "clean-up" would not be the best guarantee for maintaining the cohesion of NATO.

The boundaries of the possible

The concept of a transatlantic division of labor on defense between the United States and Europe is not farfetched. Some combination of the geographical and functional approaches, whereby ESDP would focus on peacekeeping in the Balkans and the long-term stabilization of the continent, is attractive because it does seem to reflect, at first glance, some structural features of the transatlantic relationship, as well as some emerging trends of the Alliance security debate. Assuming that "Americans are from Mars and Europeans from Venus" (arguably a disputed assumption as seen above), and the European Union's priority is to secure its neighborhood to ensure prosperity on the continent, while the United States needs to engage forces to reduce immediate threats to the safety of its citizens and ensure the continuation of its global commitments, does it not make sense to let both parties focus on what they are supposed to do best?

Such are the reasons why there is bound to be *some* division of labor on crisis management between the United States and Europe. The European Union replacing NATO for peace support in Macedonia is an example that might become a precedent, driven by a convergence of objective interests. The European Union will devote significant efforts to Africa just as the United States takes particular attention to Latin America. And there are other security policy areas where the concept will apply and can be fruitful. There is already a *de facto* division of labor between the United States and Europe in dealing with so-called rogue States such as Iran, Iraq and North Korea: in a broad generalization, one can say that, when dealing with these three hard cases, U.S. leaders are often more prone to discuss sanctions and the use of military force, whereas Europe emphasizes negotiations and dialogue. Such role-playing or "good-cop-bad-cop" policies can be helpful—provided of course that they entail a close consultation and cooperation between allies, if only to avoid the countries concerned to play allies against one another.[41]

But that is about as far as it will go. Both realities and ambitions will stand in the way of the definition of a clear division of labor between allies and/or organizations. Only in the minds and writings of scholars and analysts is it possible to devise neat schemes dividing security responsibilities the way it has been done in the above analysis. Politics do not work that way, and reality, as always, will be messy. A cynical view would be that neither the United States nor Europe has enough confidence in each other to leave the management of entire parts of their security interests to the other side: the United States is a superpower, and will want to remain engaged in Europe; the European Union has global economic and political interests, and will want to become a full-fledged military power; neither of the two will want to leave to the other the management of entire regions, or systematically defer to the other for whole areas of expertise. A more positive view is that, on the other hand, the United States and the European Union have enough common interests that they will be more naturally drawn towards attempting to work together rather than defining clear-cut, separate areas of responsibility; recent studies have confirmed that there remains a strong commonality in perceptions of security stakes in public opinions on both sides of the Atlantic.[42] Hence the intrinsic political limits of an otherwise intellectually attractive concept.

Notes:

1. John C. Hulsman, The Guns of Brussels: Burden Sharing and Power Sharing with Europe, *The Policy Review* (Internet version), June 2000.

2. In 1951, General Eisenhower, the first commander of NATO forces, said that *"If in ten years, all American troops stationed in Europe for national defense purposes have not been returned to the United States, then the whole project will have failed"* See Louis Galambos, ed., The Papers of Dwight D. Eisenhower, vol. 12, NATO and the Campaign of 1952 (Baltimore: Johns Hopkins University Press, 1989), pp. 76-77.

3. See Stanley F. Sloan, The U.S. and Transatlantic Burdensharing, Les Notes de l'IFRI—n°12 (Paris: Institut Français des Relations Internationales, 1999), p. 12.

4. Organization for Economic Cooperation and Development (OECD), 2000. In terms of percentage of Gross Domestic Product (GDP), the European Union spends about 0.33% (and plans to increase it to 0.39%), the U.S. about 0.10% (with a view to increase it to 0.13%). The Europeans finance 33% of the aid to the Middle East (50% for Palestinian territories), 40% of the reconstruction effort in Bosnia-Herzegovina, and 60% of the aid to Russia and the former Soviet Republics.

5. The EU share of the UN core budget is 37%, the U.S. share is 22%. For UN funds and special programs, the EU share is 50%, while the U.S. share is 17%. Data on UN burden-sharing provided in Malcolm Chalmers, "The Atlantic burden-sharing debate—widening or fragmenting?," International Affairs, vol. 77, no. 3, July 2001.

6. On issues of burden-sharing in the Balkans see for instance NATO Burdensharing After Enlargement, U.S. Congressional Budget Office, August 2001, Chapter 1; and Jacques Beltran and Frédéric Bozo (ed.), Etats-Unis—Europe (ed.): Réinventer l'Alliance, Travaux et Recherches de l'IFRI (Paris: Institut Français des Relations Internationales, 2001), pp. 95-96.

7. U.S. Department of Defense, Report on Allied Contributions to the Common Defense, June 2002.

8. ESDP is formally part of the EU's Common Foreign and Security Policy (CFSP), thus the limits of what "ESDP" is precisely about are hard to define. For the purposes of this paper, ESDP refers mostly to crisis management, other dimensions of the EU's security policy (such as exports control, non-proliferation, etc.) being considered the realm of CFSP *per se*. The development of ESDP is explained elsewhere in this volume. Broadly speaking, one can say that ESDP is simultaneously (a) a natural

spin-off of the European integration process, and in particular the logical corollary of the development of the CFSP, giving added credibility ("teeth") to the EU's foreign policy (b) an insurance policy in case the United States did not want to engage forces in an operation on the continent (with reference to the withdrawal of U.S. forces from operation *Sharp Guard* in 1994 and the heated debates at the end of 1995 about whether or not the U.S. should be part of post-Dayton peace-keeping in the Balkans), and (c), as stated above, a way to ensure the continuation of the U.S. engagement by demonstrating European willingness to do more for the management of security on the continent, thus more "burden-sharing."

9. Robert Hunter, The European Security and Defense Policy—NATO's Companion, or Competitor? (Santa Monica: Rand, 2002), p. 169.

10. To be fair, making operation *Enduring Freedom* a NATO operation would have taken much more time.

11. Hulsman, op. cit.

12. The NATO Council explicitly agreed in October 2001 to *"backfill selected Allied assets in NATO's area of responsibility that are required to directly support operations against terrorism"* (Statement to the Press by NATO Secretary General, October 4, 2001).

13. The concept of "subsidiarity" is widely employed in the debate about the role of the Union vis-à-vis its members: it means that the Union is supposed to take precedence over States only in areas where it can be more efficient than the States.

14. See for instance Göteborg Statement, Summit of the United States of America and the European Union, June 14, 2001.

15. Anatol Lieven, "Europe's defense begins at home," The Financial Times, 8 September 2002.

16. Chalmers, op. cit., p. 576.

17. One of the ways NATO solved this conundrum at that time was to place greater emphasis on the role of theatre nuclear weapons in Europe; hopefully, there is no credible scenario today in which NATO would need nuclear deterrence to face conventional aggression in Europe, even with reduced U.S. forces.

18. According to a study conducted in 2002 by the Chicago Council on Foreign Relations and the U.S. German Marshall Fund, China is one of the few issues where European and American public opinions strongly diverge, with 56% of Americans seeing this as a "critical" issue while only

19% of Europeans consider it "extremely important" (Worldviews 2002, findings available at www.worldviews.org).

19. Bush-Schröder Statement on Transatlantic Vision for 21st Century, March 29, 2001.

20. To be sure, one might argue that the EU has contradictory aspirations and what one may call a "Goldilocks approach" to the backfilling concept: one the one hand, they want to show that ESDP is operational and stand ready to replace NATO when and where needed—e.g. Macedonia; on the other, they fear that a failure of the Macedonia operation would ruin the credibility of the nascent ESDP and, most importantly, do not want the U.S. to take precedent from this operation to withdraw from other common operations . . . The U.S. itself is not exempt from its own contradictions here, since it both seeks to be relieved of some of the Balkans burdens without ESDP becoming a dominant option in European security. As Robert Hunter says, *"U.S. reluctance to share such risks and tasks, especially in the Balkans, the most serious area of instability in today's Europe, would be incompatible with an effort to keep ESDP as simply a second-choice option for dealing with crisis and conflict in Europe"* (Hunter, op. cit., p. 151).

21. I am indebted to Michael Quinlan for that point.

22. See Michael Cooper, "Cheney Urges Rethinking use of U.S. Ground Forces in Bosnia and Kosovo," *New York Times*, September 1, 2000, p. A16.

23. Quoted in Michael R. Gordon, "The 2000 Campaign: The Military; Bush Would Stop U.S. Peacekeeping in Balkan Fights," *New York Times*, 21 October 2000, p. A1.

24. The U.S. permanent military presence in Europe has been reduced by about two-thirds as compared to what it was at the peak of the Cold War (100,000 vs. 300,000). Some have pointed out the resistance of the U.S. Army to further reduce its forces on the continent, in particular because, allegedly, EUCOM involves the most prestigious command posts and billets. However, peacekeeping in Europe seems to be considered a valuable and rewarding enterprise in Army circles.

25. A recent and eloquent defense of the "divergence of interests" thesis is Robert Kagan, "Power and Weakness," Policy Review, June-July 2002. For views favourable to the "partnership" concept see, inter alia, David C. Gompert and F. Stephen Larrabee (ed.), America and Europe: A partnership for a new era, RAND Studies in Policy Analysis, Cambridge, Cambridge University Press, 1997; and Robert Blackwill, Report of the Task Force on The Future of Transatlantic Relations, Council on Foreign Relations, 1999. Also see Ivo H. Daalder: *"ESDP should be as relevant for*

Africa and East Timor as it is for Albania and Kosovo. Failure to make clear that ESDP's horizon stretches beyond Europe may stimulate a dangerous American belief that it is possible for Europe and the United States to form a division of labour, with the EU being responsible for Europe and the United States for the rest of the world " (A U.S. View of European Security and Defense Policy, The Brookings Institution, 2001).

26. Worldviews 2002, op. cit.

27. Hunter, op. cit., p. 141.

28. 72% Europeans vs. 48% Americans (Worldviews 2002, op. cit).

29. *"It is limited to the peacekeeping and humanitarian tasks that are set out"* (UK Prime Minister Tony Blair, Press Conference at Camp David, February 23, 2001)

30. For instance, one of the four scenarios presented by the EU Military Staff at the Ecouen Council meeting of 2000 explicitly envisioned the "separation by force of belligerent parties."

31. On this topic see for instance Nina Graeger, Henrik Larsen, Hanna Ojanen, The ESDP and the Nordic Countries—Four Variations on a Theme, The Finnish Institute of International Affairs & Institut für Europäische Politik, 2002.

32. See Willem Van Eekelen, Debating European Security, 1948-1998 (The Hague/Brussels: SDU/CEPS, 1998), in particular p. 127, which makes clear that "peacemaking" had to be understood as "peace enforcement."

33. The French view was well articulated by then-defense minister Richard in July 2001: *"Does [the development of a European reaction force] open the way for a division of labour with the U.S. taking care of the high end of the risk and conflict spectrum, and the Europeans focusing on the fire brigade function of local peace restoration in their vicinity ? I believe such a division of labour, whether intended or accidental, would damage transatlantic relations and reduce our overall capacity to deter and manage new crises."* (Security in the 21st Century—a European Perspective. Statement by Minister of Defense Alain Richard at the Center for International and Strategic Studies, Washington, July 9, 2001).

34. Worldviews 2002, op. cit.

35. Only after the UN hostages crisis (and a change in government in France) did NATO heads of State and government take a different stance, including France, the Netherlands and the UK in deciding to set up a so-called "rapid reaction force."

36. Paul Cornish and Geoffrey Edwards, "Beyond the EU-NATO dichotomy: the beginnings of a European strategic culture," International Affairs, vol. 77, n°3, July 2001, p. 598.

37. Such resentment has been fuelled in the past by situations like the reconstruction of Bosnia, where in many cases U.S. firms benefited from contracts awarded with EU funds.

38. A good analysis of U.S. expectations of ESDP is provided by Stanley R. Sloan, *The United States and European Defense*, Chaillot Paper 39, Institute for Security Studies of WEU, April 2000.

39. Kori Schake, Constructive Duplication: Reducing EU reliance on U.S. military assets (London: Center for European Reform, 2001), p. 28.

40. Speech in Washington DC by French Defense Minister Alain Richard, February 3, 2001, quoted in Hunter, op. cit., p. 141.

41. The EU visit to North Korea in 2000, during the Swedish presidency of the Union, is a case in point. It came at a time where there was no official dialogue between the Bush administration and Pyong-Yang. However, it seems that there were no close consultations between Brussels and Washington before the trip.

42. See Worldviews 2002, op. cit.

A European View of the U.S. and ESDP

Peter van Ham

Introduction

After the atrocities of 11 September 2001, NATO and the European Union (EU) are engaged in a confrontation with international terrorism. This is not just a war, but a "just war" against an enemy whose willingness to use asymmetrical warfare poses new challenges to the West and global security.

This chapter asks how the EU has responded to the 9-11 events and their aftermath, especially focussing on the consequences for Europe's ambitions to develop a Common Foreign and Security Policy (CFSP) and a European Security and Defense Policy (ESDP). It also examines the consequences of America's new strategic priorities—shifting away from Europe and focusing on the Global War On Terrorism (GWOT) and regime change in Iraq—for the EU's role as a security actor. Finally, it asks how the new security environment affects the transatlantic relationship.

EU: Supporting the reluctant sheriff

Under the Bush administration, Washington has followed a "yes, but"-approach, encouraging the EU's geostrategic ambitions under the condition that the U.S. remains fully involved, if not always in charge. Especially after 9-11, the U.S. no longer seems too keen to use its diplomatic and military clout to broker new deals in other slumbering Balkan disputes. The "management" of European security is now largely in the hands of Europeans themselves. This was also suggested by the EU itself, since a Joint Declaration two days after the terrorist attacks argued that the CFSP and ESDP should be strengthened, "ensuring that the Union is genuinely capable of speaking out clearly and doing so in one voice."[1] But still, the main question is whether the EU and its member states will be able (and willing) to rise to this occasion.

The EU has gone out of its way to support the U.S. and has explicitly labelled the 9-11 attacks "an assault on our open, democratic, tolerant and multicultural societies. (. . .) The European Union will cooperate with the United States in bringing to justice and punishing the perpetrators, sponsors and accomplices of such barbaric acts. On the basis of [UN] Security Council Resolution 1368, a riposte by the U.S. is legitimate. The Member States of the Union are prepared to undertake such actions, each according to its means."[2] In this case, "each according to its means" implied that some countries were mobilising or offering troops, others providing intelligence or making available air bases.

The EU agreed on a number of internal security issues, such as the EU-wide search and arrest warrant, new extradition procedures, agreement on data-sharing and a more prominent role of Europol (the EU's nascent law enforcement organization) and Eurojust (the future European unit for cooperation between national prosecuting authorities).[3] The U.S. has also requested (and generally received) assistance from the EU in police and judicial cooperation, in particular regarding regulations on extradition and police surveillance. Washington is also interested in more direct access to the EU's Schengen Information System (SIS). The European Commission introduced EU-wide standards to improve security for air travellers as well as emergency legislation to "freeze" more than 100 million worth of assets of people suspected of terrorism. The Commission also tabled proposals for a common definition of terrorism and for a system of EU-wide penalties for terrorist offences. It proposed measures reinforcing the security features of the common visa and is exploring how existing EU legislation on asylum and financial markets can be made "terrorism proof."

Commission President Prodi suggested in October 2001, that "recent events have shown the need for *more*—not less—action at the EU level."[4] But despite these good plans for consorted future EU policies, few member states have been waiting for the Union's heralded Mr. CFSP (Javier Solana) to forge a common European reaction in the foreign policy, security and defense field. Compared to the European Commission's active and rapid involvement in fighting international terrorism, Solana's role remained low-key. Behind the scenes, Solana has been working hard on intra-Western coalition maintenance, and U.S. Secretary of State Colin Powell reportedly dials "Europe's" telephone number several times a week. Solana has also been going back and forth to the Middle East trying to avoid a further escalation of the Israeli-Palestinian confrontation.

Nevertheless, it has been the EU's big players—Germany, France and the UK—who have dominated most of the post-9-11 action and the media, making it clear that at times of a serious crisis national responses still easily override the rhetoric of European solidarity and cooperation. Mr. Prodi has tried to put a nice face on the lack of a forceful CFSP, arguing that a "common policy is not, of course, the same thing as a single policy uniformly adopted by every Member State. No: a common policy pools the different strengths of different individual countries, enabling them to pursue shared goals using shared instruments."[5] In that sense the EU indeed follows a "common policy," with every member state doing its thing and formulating its own historically informed answers. This applies to both the "European" answer to fighting the GWOT as well as the key question of how to handle the Iraqi problem.

During the first few months after 9-11, this slipshod EU coordination of foreign, security and defense issues was tolerable since the policy parameters for member states remained narrow. In all EU countries, the atmosphere of loyalty put pressure on traditionally critical voices of U.S. military actions to toe the line of the new Bush doctrine: "You're either for us, or against us" in the global anti-terrorism campaign. However, behind this front of solidarity, different voices and tones were already making themselves heard within the European choir. The longer the GWOT was dragging on, the more vocal these alternative and critical voices were becoming. Now that the image of a crumbling World Trade Center is fading and being replaced by pictures of anarchy in Kabul and a looming war in and over Iraq, the disquiet that was mounting behind the scenes now becomes more outspoken and public.

It has become clear that a core group of the EU's Big Powers will increasingly offer leadership to any European CFSP and ESDP worthy of their acronyms. But this core-group leadership also puts pressure on the EU's cohesion, raising doubts about Europe's capability and willingness for unified action. As Dominique Moïsi argued, "[t]here is a re-nationalization of foreign policy, because it is a matter of different capabilities and feelings of interest. This is a litmus test for Europe."[6] Since the EU's Big Powers also amongst themselves disagree on their relationship with the U.S. (culminating in the question of Iraqi disarmament and/or regime change), it should be clear that the very idea of a cohesive and effective EU is now seriously questioned.

For Europe, one of the main questions is what to do with an America that doesn't want to listen to its former allies, mainly because it doesn't have to. It now becomes increasingly clear that for U.S. foreign policy, the Next Big Idea may well be that of "Empire," which, as Robert D. Kaplan has argued, is "in some ways the most benign form of order."[7] Nevertheless, this emerging *Pax Americana* inevitably will be a fragile global order, since it carries all its eggs in one basket. For Europe—and the rest of the world—it's an uneasy gamble that the U.S. system will prove to be wise and generous beyond belief. It would therefore be preferable for Europe to make itself heard and to draw a clear line in the sand against American dominance. Not in pursuit of some old-fashioned and useless *Realpolitik* of "balancing," but to restrain the development of a U.S.-dominated world order. Such a *Pax Americana* would not be in the European interest. For historical and geopolitical reasons, Europeans emphasize the role and value of international law and institutions and cherish a broader definition of security than most American policymakers. This is reflected in different approaches to the United Nations, the Kyoto Protocol, the International Criminal Court (ICC) and the security aspects of foreign aid and assistance. Although the proverbial Martian observer might consider these differences trivial, they are a cause of significantly different strategic visions among allies, and hence negatively affect the very idea of a cohesive "West."

Iraq as a litmus test

The handling of Iraq is turning into a trial for America's worldwide responsibility as the security guarantor of last resort. But what most Europeans consider to be the problems and drawbacks of a military intervention in Iraq—the lack of a clear legal basis in international law, the precedent of a "pre-emptive strike," and the further exacerbation of violence in the region—many Americans refuse to consider as serious obstacles to decisive military action.

With the notable exception of British prime minister Tony Blair, European leaders fear that they will be drawn into a big and awful adventure in Iraq, which will be beyond their control. German Bundeskanzler Gerhard Schröder has clearly rejected his country's participation in an Iraqi invasion, which has put significant strain on the otherwise excellent German-American relationship. France, a permanent member of the UN Security Council, also has different ideas about the handling of Iraq, agreeing on disarmament but not "regime change."

No number of persuasive European arguments seems to be able to sway President Bush that Saddam Hussein can be dealt with without using a big stick. Part of the problem here is that European heedings and criticism are not judged on their own merits, but have already been classified under the heading of "EUnuch complaints." In its mild form it reflects the widely held U.S. opinion (most compellingly formulated by Kagan in his *Policy Review*-piece)[8] that Europeans favour non-military solutions and are willing to embark upon endless negotiations simply because they are militarily weak, and not because they deem these policies ethically superior or more effective (be it, perhaps, only in the long-term). Kagan argues that "When the European great powers were strong, they believed in strength and martial glory. Now, they see the world through the eyes of weaker powers.[9]

But European concerns and criticism are also often construed as another sign of anti-Americanism and lack of loyalty to the U.S. in times of crisis. This may be somewhat surprising, especially since senior members of the U.S. Congress also urged some caution before any military action is undertaken. But it is especially the neoconservative elite which considers the European penchant for multilateralism a ploy to frustrate American foreign policy objectives. As Jeffrey Gedmin has argued: "[Multilateralism] is the codeword for leveraging up the medium-sized EU and chaining down the mightly Americans. It's a European obsession that is unlikely to go away."[10] Here, American contempt for a (militarily) weak Europe is linked to a general suspicion of European intentions. It also means that when European politicians call for a "rule-based global order," Washington may (correctly) understand this as a rejection of the rising *Pax Americana*.

This atmosphere of mutual misunderstanding has the potential to erode the foundations of the transatlantic security relationship. The key question now is how this problem should be handled?

Room for improvement and compromise

Critical but constructive analysts of the transatlantic troubles tend to come up with two solutions. First, the U.S. must use its unprecedented power wisely and with restraint. For example, Josef Joffe suggests that "[a]s long as the United States continues to provide international public goods while resisting the lure of unilateralism, envy and resentment will not escalate into fear and loathing." His advice to Washington would therefore be: "Pursue your interests by serving the interests of others. Transform dependents into stakeholders. Turn America the Ubiquitous into America the Indispensable."[11] Second, Europe (and NATO/EU in particular) must make itself more relevant to the U.S. and be both capable and willing to take on the serious military challenge of fighting international terrorism. Europe should therefore be investing more in defense and adopt a more martial attitude to addressing global problems. Lord Robertson is the most eloquent exponent of this way of thinking. It also implies (as Richard N. Haass, Director of the Policy Planning Staff of the U.S. Department of State, has argued), that "America and Europe must reorient their focus and energies beyond the borders of Europe."[12] Here, a stronger and more effective ESDP is seen as the redeemer of both NATO and the transatlantic security relationship in general.

Surely, this is well-meant advice, which assumes that although Americans may be from Mars and Europeans from Venus, their courses and discourses should meet. Both pieces of advice are also on the mark and politically wise and expedient. But this doesn't mean that either Washington or Europe will actually follow them. Western Europe's leaders are faced with a public opinion which doesn't go along with an American assault on Iraq in the absence of a clear UN Security Council mandate, and certainly is reluctant to lend the U.S. any concrete military support without such a clear political and legal basis. Even Prime Minister Blair faces tough domestic opposition to Britain's political and military support to the U.S.. As former British Chief of Defense Staff Field Marshall Lord Bramall formulated it: "You don't have licence to attack someone else's country just because you don't like the leadership."[13] Obviously, what many Americans see as a pre-emptive attack in self-defense, many Europeans see as risky American military adventurism.

The American handling of Iraq will show whether Washington still takes European allies seriously, and whether Europeans, in turn, deserve to be taken seriously. But now that things may well be on the road to getting bloody in Iraq, it remains doubtful whether a U.S.-European compromise and meeting of minds will come about in time. The central question here is what consequences this will have for Europe's role as a foreign policy actor and how these developments affect the transatlantic relationship.

In a mood of iconoclastic thinking, EU Trade Commissioner Pascal Lamy recently asked himself "how far will Europeans go to defend their rule-based systems? Will we take risks, lose lives and pay more? That's the real question, which we Europeans have carefully organized ourselves not to ask."[14] Put differently: are European public opinion and policymakers prepared to accept the role as permanent sidekicks to the emerging American hegemon, or will Europe decide to play a more independent role and at times even challenge the U.S.? These questions can now no longer be dodged, but deserve to be faced head-on. We should therefore be couragous enough to ask ourselves whether a more competitive U.S.-European strategic relationship might not be more realistic and, perhaps, even healthier than the crumbling myth (and sometimes farce) of a continued "post-post-post-Cold War" transatlantic security community?

Common sense and a mixture of trepidation and ostrich attitude, have kept most Europeans from even considering a transatlantic decoupling. Even today, Europeans are much more keen to re-invent, modernize, restructure (and what not) NATO than Americans, which again demonstrates that an operational transatlantic security relationship is more important to Europe than the U.S.. But the difficult road towards a now likely Iraqi invasion may well open European eyes and concentrate their minds to focus on what is left of the fundamentals of the Atlantic strategic community.

What matters is whether the U.S. will take NATO and the EU seriously as organizations, or whether it will turn to individual European states and make bilateral arrangements. What matters is whether key European states will act together (most likely within the appropriate EU fora), formulating their security policies as a group and willing and able to negotiate and cooperate with the U.S. on that basis. On both issues, recent events don't bode well: The

U.S. obviously prefers to deal with London and Paris, rather than with "Brussels." Moreover, Europeans tend to budge when faced with massive U.S. political pressure, as was the case with the British and Italian willingness to consider offering immunity to U.S. soldiers even if this would go against the spirit (if not necessarily the letter) of the ICC.

Whereas Kagan is right that the European continent is largely pacified and on a multilateralist binge, he is, however, wrong to assume that this is a permanent situation which the U.S. can take for granted. On the contrary, if Washington continues to cherry-pick its allies within Europe, this practice would seriously undermine the dynamics of Europe's security and defense integration, with detrimental consequences not only for the EU, but for NATO as well. Like any experiment, the "Europe project" is highly susceptible to outside influences. Institutions need to be used; if not, they'll either wither away or—as we now see with NATO—change their spots beyond recognition to remain desperately in the security business. The results are unlikely to be satisfactory.

The EU should consider "Iraq" a crisis in the Chinese sense of the word: a risk *and* an opportunity. Given the major political and economic consequences of a Middle Eastern conflagration, Europe will be seriously affected and hence become involved one way or other. At the same time, European states should realize that it is crunch-time for their security and defense project, and be willing to seize the Iraq crisis as an opportunity to galvanize a clear, European approach *vis-à-vis* the U.S.. But just as 9-11 has strengthened a national, rather than a European (or NATO) approach, it has proved difficult to arrive at such a consorted European policy. The likelihood that EU member states will actually rally around their famous blue flag remains difficult to predict; there are (too) many moving parts and uncertainties at the moment. Much would also depend on how long and bloody the Iraqi conflict may turn out, and how, and to what extent, it will affect and spill-over towards Israel, Saudi Arabia and other hot-spots. Since Russia has also spoken out clearly against a military option to get rid of Saddam Hussein, a policy conflict with Moscow should also be reckoned with.

Conclusion: The necessity of strenghtening ESDP

Given the high stakes at hand, it is now time for European states to determine what they want to achieve with their EU-project. Just as the coming year will be decisive for NATO's future as a serious and effective defense organization, the handling of Iraq will set the tone for the EU's foreign, security and defense policies. Now that the European Convention on the future of the Union is in full swing and due to present its suggestions for institutional reform in Spring 2003, the notion of a more independent European defense should be seriously considered and thought through. Since the EU is often (and rightfully) blamed for its inability to think geopolitically and strategically, serious progress towards a EU Defense White Paper is required. Although the European Commission has already initiated a series of experts meetings to come up with ideas, options and scenarios for an effective CFSP and ESDP, just another fancy document will, of course, not be sufficient. What is required is a change of mindset based on the realization that Europe is becoming a major global actor in its own right, whether it likes it or not. This means that on top of the expert report due to be published jointly with the Convention's first results, EU member states have to go through the process of rethinking their collective foreign policy, security and defense priorities. Ideally, this should result in a clear and practical European military doctrine.

Inevitably, these EU-policies will now be outlined in contrast to America's unilateralist and military approach to international problems and conflicts. This should hardly come as a surprise since it nicely confirms the Mars/Venus cliché of transatlantic relations. For America today, the guiding principle is to do what is in its national interest and then see if you can convince others, either by words or by deeds. The EU should try to emulate this approach, with the added clause that the concept of "European interests" by definition accommodates a modicum of reduced sovereignty in exhange for a number of public goods like institutions and treaties. This naturally includes the "public good" of a relevant and functioning transatlantic security relationship. Focussing on the EU's "continental interests" may have the added benefit of kick-starting the long overdue process of "strategic thinking": How does the EU (as an organization, not as a loose group of member states) interpret its strengths, weaknesses, opportunities and threats, and how does it optimalize its interests in this context? But by emulating America's focus on its own interests, Europeans should have both a clear conscience and a political *carte blanche*: they can not be blamed if transatlantic relations may (temporarily) worsen and even escalate.

Being aware of the risks involved, one of the biggest challenges for EU-policymakers and European leaders is to make sure that transatlantic security troubles are kept in quarantine, and have as little chance as possible to infect the trade, economic and financial ties between the U.S. and Europe. Surely, this will fail too, but preferably as little as possible. But here, too, as much of the task and responsibility of damage-limitation rests with Washington as with Brussels. It will also mean that the EU will have a special responsibility to go beyond a foreign and security policy of "just say No" to American solutions. This implies that Europe will have to offer viable alternatives every time it decides to disagree with Washington. In the Iraq case, the European consensus has been that a strict UN inspection regime should be forced upon Saddam Hussein to give surety that no WMD-programmes are actually under way. This has been a constructive approach, emphasizing the necessity to obtain the UN's blessing before any military action would be undertaken.

What would be the desired objective of such a step towards more European political and security autonomy? I do not consider it either a risky or a courageous enterprise. Europe has little to lose now that NATO no longer functions as it should: other alternatives like muddling through and riding the coat-tails of U.S. supremacy are equally unattractive. All this makes an "EU-option" the only credible one left. There is even a chance that, in the end, the U.S. may decide that European political opinions are worth listening to. Since most American policymakers today are self-proclaimed Realists, all assuming that power and naked self-interest determine the dynamics and outcome of international politics, Washington will not be really surprised that the EU—with all its economic and political might—finally chooses to chart its own foreign and security policies and is prepared to stick to its course. It also does not mean that the EU will become a bulwark of anti-Americanism, at least not any more than that Washington could be blamed for being anti-European.

The outcome of such a (possible) strategic decoupling would be a temporary transatlantic rift. It would certainly be more serious than a sandbox spat, but it would not have to be too dramatic. In the end, the transatlantic cat will land on her feet, losing perhaps one of her lives, but gaining another one: A transatlantic security relationship based on the realization that with the end of the Cold War and after 9-11, Europe and the U.S. will work together, side by side if possible, to address common challenges and work out common problems. But there will be times when opinions will legitimately differ, when interests and perceptions will not coalesce. Optimists will hope that the emerging strategic divide is transitory rather than structural. I am not one of them. But even if the transatlantic meeting of minds and strategic interests will come about in the near future, NATO's centrality as the Euro-American security pivot is unlikely to be restored. European and American interests usually overlap, but are every so often also at variance. It's about time to acknowledge this openly and work around the most glaring and painful controversies.

Notes:

1. "Joint Declaration by Heads of State and Government, President of the EP, President of the Commission and the High Representative for the CFSP." 14 September 2001.

2. "Conclusions and Plan of Action of the Extraordinary Council Meeting on 21 September 2001." Press Release 140/01.

3. See Joanna Apap, "Common European instruments to tackle terrorism," *CEPS Commentary* (September 2001). To be found at http://www.cepts.be/Commentary/September01/terrorism.htm

4. Speech of Romano Prodi, President of the European Commission, "Preparation of the Ghent European Council," Press conference, 18 October 2001. (Emphasis in the original).

5. Speech of Romano Prodi, President of the European Commission, "Time for real solidarity," to the European Parliament, 24 October 2001.

6. Quoted in Peter Ford, "Common foreign policy still eludes unified Europe," *Christian Science Monitor*, 22 October 2001.

7. Quoted in Emily Eakin, "All roads lead to D.C.," *The New York Times*, 31 March 2002.

8. Robert Kagan, "Power and weakness," in *Policy Review*, no. 113 (June 2002). [http://www.policyreview.org/JUN02/kagan.html] (7 October 2002).

9. Kagan, "Power and weakness." Online.

10. Jeffrey Gedmin, "The Alliance is doomed," *The Washington Post*, 20 May 2002.

11. Josef Joffe, "Who's afraid of Mr. Big?," *The National Interest*, no. 64 (Summer 2001), p. 52.

12. Ambassador Richard N. Haass, "Charting a new course in the transatlantic relationship," Center for European Reform (London), 10 June 2002.

13. Quoted in "Doves launch last-ditch campaign for Gulf peace," *The Observer* (London), 11 August 2002.

14. Quoted in Steven Erlanger, "America the invulnerable? The world looks again," *The New York Times*, 21 July 2002.

American Views of European Security and Defense Policy

Daniel Hamilton

American political leaders and security experts are ambivalent about the European Union's project to build a European Security and Defense Policy—to the extent that they are paying attention to it at all.

For the past half-century U.S. political leaders have expressed support, with varying degrees of enthusiasm, for a more cohesive Europe that could act, effectively and confidently, as America's partner on the European continent and in the wider world. Yet when Europeans have actually moved to establish truly "common" foreign security and defense policies, they have often been faced with American concerns that such coherence may become inward-looking and exclusive, or based on "lowest-common-denominator" consensus-building within the EU, and thus weaken the primacy of the NATO Alliance or impede US leadership and freedom of maneuver.

American ambivalence is reflected in the official attitude of both the Clinton and Bush Administrations toward ESDP, which has been that of conditional support. The Clinton Administration's support was conditioned by what Secretary of State Madeleine Albright termed the "three D's:" no *discrimination* against non-EU NATO members, no *decoupling* of European and North American security, and no *duplication* of NATO's operational planning system or its command structure ("no duplication" was never defined nor intended to mean that the EU should not develop certain capabilities that already existed in the Alliance; indeed much of the Clinton Administration's efforts, such as the NATO Defense Capability Initiative, sought to prod the Europeans into developing precisely such capabilities. This distinction has been lost on many analysts).[1]

The Clinton Administration used these concerns to frame and guide its support for a more cohesive and responsive European foreign policy and above all, for more capable European defense. The Kosovo war affirmed to American leaders that not enough European armed forces were ready for the diverse, rapidly-evolving challenges of the post-Cold War world. In American eyes Europe has been sluggish in its efforts to manage the shift away from the massed, terrain-based forces necessary for the Cold War toward more mobile, deployable and sustainable forces and improved lift, logistics and intelligence capabilities. Kosovo underscored European dependence on the U.S. for precision-strike capability, surveillance and intelligence assets, refueling, lift, and high-end command and control systems.

Republican political leaders who were openly skeptical and even scornful of ESDP during the Clinton years have, since joining the Bush Administration, essentially continued the Clinton Administration's approach of conditional support tied to pressure for improved European military capabilities. President Bush basically reiterated the three D's during his first meeting with other NATO heads of state and government in Brussels on June 13, 2001:

> We agreed that NATO and the European Union must work in common purpose. It is in NATO's interest for the European Union to develop a rapid reaction capability. A strong, capable European force integrated with NATO would give us more options for handling crises when NATO, as a whole, chooses not to engage. NATO must be generous in the help it gives the EU. *And similarly, the EU must welcome participation by NATO allies who are not members of the EU. And we must not waste scarce resources, duplicating effort or working at cross purposes.*[2]

Official U.S. support for ESDP has been consistent, but it remains shallow. In part it reflects the domestic American struggle between a number of different perspectives on ESDP. Any attempt to characterize such views as different "schools of thought" inevitably risks giving the debate more coherence and prominence than it really has, and also risks downplaying the considerable overlap that exists between some of these perspectives. Nonetheless, drawing out such distinctions may help to illuminate different ways American opinion leaders think about the issue.

ESDP supporters are primarily centrist Democrats and Republicans who believe that the United States needs a strong and coherent European Union as a partner on the European continent and beyond.[3] They are concerned by Europe's relative weakness, and believe that U.S.-European power asymmetries are not healthy for either side. They believe that American popular support for a continuing U.S. role in Europe is related to the perception that America's European allies are willing and able to assume more responsibility not only for their own security but also for defending common interests of the transatlantic community in the wider world, and see ESDP as a possible expression of that commitment. They accept that common foreign and security policy is a logical next step in the European integration process and can help to avoid renationalization of European defense. They support ESDP as an initiative to improve European capabilities that, if developed with care, can also be mutually reinforcing with such NATO initiatives as the Prague Summit capability commitments and the nascent NATO Response Force.

Supporters also believe that ESDP could equip the EU to assume the lead in the Balkans or to engage, if necessary, in areas such as Africa, where the US is unlikely to play a prominent role. They believe the United States should welcome a European capability for crisis management in situations where NATO—meaning, in practice, the United States—would decide not to become engaged. They welcome the EU's civilian Headline Goals, as set forth at the June 2000 Feira and June 2001 Göteborg European Council meetings, that EU member states should by 2003 be able to make available up to 5,000 police officers (of which 1,000 within 30 days) for EU contributions led by international organizations (UN or OSCE) or for autonomous EU missions; provide up to 200 experts in the rule of law field; establish a pool of experts to undertake civilian administrative tasks; and make available civil protection intervention teams of up to 2,000 persons that can be deployed at very short notice.

Looking to future challenges, supporters believe ESDP and the EU's Common Foreign and Security Policy (CFSP) could be vehicles for both U.S.-EU and NATO-EU efforts to counter terrorism and weapons of mass destruction and to cooperate in civil emergency disaster relief, humanitarian relief and information security—all potential elements of collaboration under what one might term "transatlantic homeland security." In short, supporters believe that if ESDP and CFSP are developed and implemented properly, they can be vehicles for a stronger, outward-looking Europe and a more balanced, global partnership with the United States.

Skeptics include conservative Atlanticists and many members of Congress, who question the wisdom of ESDP and the prospects of its success. They do not believe that the Europeans have the will or the wallet to achieve their goals. They are weary of repeated European capability pledges that go unfulfilled. They are concerned that ESDP could lead European governments to close or restrict European arms markets to U.S. competition. In short, they believe ESDP at best to be a meddlesome distraction from more serious security challenges and at worst to be a pernicious effort to counter U.S. influence. They believe that continuing EU-Turkish tensions over Turkey's ability to participate fully in ESDP initiatives that affect Turkish security interests are corrosive at a time when Turkey's strategic importance has grown. They doubt that the EU will ever be able to accommodate Turkish interests. Since Turkish assent is a prerequisite for the success of the broad package of cooperative elements that has been developed by NATO and EU authorities, the skeptics doubt that ESDP will ever really get off the ground, or believe that failure with Turkey could strengthen French views within EU councils, which could turn the EU away from deeper cooperation with NATO and toward more "autonomous" and duplicative ventures. According to this perspective, ESDP is simply one more example that the grand project of European integration has gone off the rails, and is being defined less in terms of positive European ideals and transatlantic partnership and more in terms of "autonomy" and as a counter to U.S. power.

While the skeptics are concerned with what they see as divisive trends, another group—one could call them "the decouplers"— believe that such divisions could benefit the transatlantic relationship. They believe that Europe is basically secure and that the U.S. faces more serious challenges elsewhere—the Greater Middle East, South Asia, and the Asia-Pacific region. They don't believe that tiresome battles with the French or Brussels bureaucrats over the arcane details of ESDP are worth their time or energy. Decouplers believe that if Europe can use ESDP to improve its own capacities and provide stability on its own continent, this could free the U.S. to devote its own energies to these other, more serious regional threats.

For the decouplers, ESDP has become a convenient excuse for American burden-shedding in Europe. Decouplers seize on European rhetorical excesses—such as the EU's declaration of "some operational capabilities" for ESDP at the Laeken European Council in December 2001—as ammunition for their domestic argument that the EU is ready and willing to take over certain U.S. responsibilities. They welcome the Bush Administration's concept of "backfilling," which would assign Europeans the prime responsibility for low-intensity missions and operations, notably in the Balkans, and thus free U.S. military forces for high-intensity combat missions, and more generally for the management of "hard" security issues, particularly in the Middle East and Asia.[4] According to this view, such "backfilling" could be the first step toward a new transatlantic "division of labor" whereby Europeans take on certain missions and Americans others. Decouplers are not numerous, but they do occupy influential positions in the upper reaches of the Pentagon and the White House, and include a number of U.S. Senators.

A fourth group are those who one might call "transformationists." They include many defense intellectuals and senior military officers. They view ESDP through the prism of the revolution in military affairs that is transforming the entire way the U.S. military approaches preparedness and warfare. This tremendous change is sparked by various factors, including massive U.S. defense spending, introduction of advanced technologies, and accompanying revolutions in communications and information industries. Transformation is not only about money, technology or capability, however. These innovations are affecting how the U.S. organizes, trains and even conceives of future warfare.

The U.S. military services are making dramatic strides to change the way they fight. They are shifting from force-oriented to capability-oriented approaches to military planning. They are shifting from attrition-based force on force warfare to effects-based operations. They are shifting from terrain-based to time-based capabilities. They are shifting from segmented land, sea and air services to joint operations. They are focusing more on asymmetric threats. The U.S. Navy's new doctrine of network-centric warfare, the U.S. Army's shift toward light, flexible and quickly deployable units that can be integrated into information networks, the U.S. Air Force's development of the global strike task force, the U.S. Marine Corps shift from intermediate staging bases to direct projection of naval combat power to onshore targets, and the creation of the Joint Forces Command to experiment with different doctrines are only a few examples of the changes underway. On top of all of this, the U.S. defense budget is approaching 400 billion dollars.[5]

Seen from this perspective, ESDP seems almost quaint — and largely irrelevant. Transformationists question whether America's European partners have truly grasped the dimensions of change underway and wonder whether they are prepared to make the decisions needed to fight alongside Americans or even to be militarily valuable partners for the United States. The 2001 U.S. Congressional Budget Office report on burden-sharing, which on the whole provides a balanced picture of European contributions, concludes that "a failure by many of NATO's European members to keep up with technological advances could render them incapable of operating alongside US forces in future military conflicts."[6]

As a result, transformationists are increasingly resigned to transatlantic military divergence. They credit common efforts to deal with past challenges, but believe that U.S. and European leaders simply have different future priorities for their military forces. They do not believe that most European governments agree on the kinds of threats or types of future wars that are driving U.S. transformation efforts, and thus are unlikely to adapt their military forces in ways that are compatible with U.S. changes. Even if there was broad agreement on future threats, tight European defense budgets will constrain European options.

According to this perspective, ESDP is not the reason for transatlantic divergence, but unless managed well it could exacerbate such trends. The ESDP focus on regional stabilization in and around Europe is a far cry from the U.S. focus on fighting in high-end combat situations anywhere in the world.[7]

In short, the transformationists believe that U.S. and European militaries are no longer looking at the same military tasks. This means that U.S. and European forces will be less able to plan, train and operate together. If this is the case, they believe, then it won't really matter whether a neat new set of NATO-EU cooperative mechanisms are agreed, because neither side will be likely to resort to them. For instance, while the U.S. has insisted that EU forces operate to NATO standards, there is a real question whether U.S. forces in future will want to operate to NATO standards.

Despite their quite different starting points, these approaches do share some common ground. All are concerned more with transatlantic tensions arising from Europe's current relative weakness than from any potential—and quite theoretical—tensions resulting from future European strength. Most believe that the U.S. should welcome deeper EU integration to the degree that it is accompanied by EU commitment to share international security and defense burdens. But even those who support ESDP's potential are concerned that European force commitments and capability pledges too often tend to be little more than empty exercises in European self-assertion. Americans across the board are weary of repeated European efforts and pledges that seem to melt away with the next spring thaw. All are skeptical whether ESDP will survive Greek-Turkish problems over Turkey's role in the ESDP decision-making process. There is also a growing perception that British ardor for ESDP has cooled, and thus that the steam has gone out of ESDP over the past year. They wonder whether it will ever recover the attention of EU leaders.

These perspectives also underscore another point. In American eyes, ESDP is not just a narrow technical topic for policy wonks. It is an issue that is emblematic of a far larger strategic debate about how—and even whether — Europe and the United States can tackle together the security challenges posed by the post-Cold War, post-911 world.

ESDP was originally intended to address challenges posed by the post-Cold War strategic transformation of the 1990s, when the grand transatlantic Alliance lost the enemy that held it together, Europe was beset by continuing turbulence across the European continent and great human tragedy in the Balkans, and western Europeans discovered that they remained unable themselves to stabilize their continent. The strategic debate at the time revolved around the question whether the United States and Europe were prepared to adapt and expand their partnership to the threats and opportunities posed by the collapse of communism and Soviet power in the eastern half of the continent. After great hemming and hawing, and tremendous human tragedy, the answer was yes. We engaged in the Balkans, we defined a new partnership with Russia, and expanded the zone of stability that once encompassed half of Europe to embrace the entire continent. In the process we deepened and broadened our partnership beyond the traditional NATO model and included closer U.S.-EU cooperation as part of a much more dense network of institutional cooperation that also spawned the EU's Common Foreign and Security Policy and the European Security and Defense Policy.

While the original Petersberg tasks guiding the development of ESDP are broad and vague enough to incorporate the full spectrum of military activity, the clear focus of ESDP's Headline Goals and accompanying activities is to equip the EU with a capacity for regional stabilization on or near its borders. Such a capacity would be a vast improvement on the EU's record during the 1990's, and should be welcomed by Americans.

Since September 11, however, Europe and America find themselves in a second post-Cold War period of strategic transformation and redefinition. The post-9ll strategic issue is whether the United States and Europe are once again prepared to adapt their partnership to address a diverse and dangerous set of challenges ranging far beyond the European continent. As this debate unfolds, there is some question in the United States how—and whether—ESDP as originally conceived will be relevant to this new agenda.

If ESDP was primarily about stabilizing the periphery of an increasingly stable Europe, can it or should it also become the vehicle to equip Europeans to act far beyond their continent? If ESDP was originally intended to make Europeans marginally more effective at policing their back yard, can it or should it be adapted to defend European societies from elusive terrorists, failed states or aggressive dictators in regions far away from the European homeland? If ESDP was originally intended to prevent future Bosnias, can it or should it be adapted to prevent future Afghanistans? Or future Iraqs?

In this volume Ralph Thiele suggests that ESDP should have not just one military purpose but two: stability operations with or without the US and advanced expeditionary warfare with the U.S. The first purpose would equip Europeans primarily for contingencies in and near Europe, or in Africa, while the latter could be for contingencies anywhere in the world where common transatlantic interests are threatened. This approach would find many American supporters—if done in ways that are mutually supportive of NATO's own efforts.

Opportunity may present itself through a synergistic relationship between the Headline Goals the EU has set for ESDP and the "Headline Goals" NATO has set for its own Response Force initiative.

The EU Headline Goal commits EU nations to be able to deploy in 2003 up to 60,000 soldiers, at 60 days' notice, for crisis management operations lasting at least a year. The European Capability Action Plan of 2001 is intended to address shortfalls along the way. This is a start, but does not cover the broadest definition of Petersberg tasks, which could include high-intensity combat missions at great distance. Most analysts doubt whether the EU would be able to field the full range of capabilities required for the broadest definition of Petersberg tasks by the end of this decade.

The NATO Response Force (NRF),[8] on the other hand, focuses on high-end capabilities. As proposed by U.S. officials, NRF would be a rotational set of air, land and sea forces capable of deploying anywhere in the world within 5 to 30 days, capable of warfighting alone if necessary for 30 days, or to serve as the initial entry force to prepare for a larger force presence. It would be capable of performing a full range of tasks, from evacuation of non-combatants to operating in a nuclear, biological, chemical or radiological environment. It would be fully joint, capable of supporting up to 200 air sorties a day, composed of a brigade-sized land force, and of maritime forces based on the NATO standing naval force, and including command and control capabilities to fully integrate into joint operations—a total of 21,000 personnel. NRF units, drawn from a larger pool of forces, would engage in rotational training cycles so that at any given time a core set of forces would be on-call, and that important transformational lessons and capabilities would be diffused more broadly. Because the concept is to build a small core and then develop from there, initial costs would be modest. Plans call for an initial operating capability by October 2004 and full capability by October 2006.

The NRF could serve as the pilot for a broader transformation of European forces and become a central focus for a transatlantic transformation process. U.S. and European forces might be able to "bypass" the capabilities gap, rather than try to close it, by integrating European forces into the key training and conceptual revolutions associated with U.S. force transformation. The U.S. should also needs partners in transformation, since much of transformation is about networking knowledge, developing better assessments, and drawing on collective expertise. In short, NRF could facilitate a process of "transatlantic transformation" that is synergistic with an ESDP focus on regional stabilization in and around Europe, especially since both projects are likely to draw on the same set of forces. Moreover, since most EU capability shortfalls are also addressed by the Prague Summit's capability commitments, any action taken by individual European nations to remedy their shortfalls will contribute to both ESDP and NRF. If the relationship between ESDP and NRF is managed badly, however, this could lead to a mutually destructive spiral that would accelerate transatlantic divergence of standards, training, and threat assessments guiding force planning and development.

In sum, the way American opinion leaders have been approaching ESDP is broadly similar to U.S. reactions to other big advances in European integration. When the Single Market initiative was launched in the 1980s, the initial U.S. reaction was skepticism. There was great doubt whether the EU really had the will to move ahead. Little attention was paid to it. When the Europeans demonstrated that they were actually serious, American commentators focused on possible negative implications of a "Fortress Europe" for U.S. commercial interests. When these concerns largely faded, there was a great and sudden burst of attention to the possibilities for American companies and U.S. interests. A similar cycle is discernible in U.S. approaches to the launch of the Euro and the creation of ESDP: initial skepticism, followed by worry about negative consequences for U.S. interests, followed by conditional support.

For most American opinion leaders who follow the issue, the details of ESDP are less important than the signal it sends about European intentions. Are Europeans willing and able to work together to align the EU's grand project of European integration with a strategic transformation of transatlantic partnership to address future challenges in and beyond Europe? And will Americans find the patience to work with an EU that is only just starting down the road of common security and defense policy? These are open questions.

Notes:

1. The three D's were outlined for the first time by Secretary Albright just days after the U.K.-French meeting at St. Malo on ESDP. See Madeleine K. Albright, "The right balance will secure NATO's future," *Financial Times*, December 7, 1998; the three D's were subsequently amended by NATO Secretary General Lord Robertson into the three "I's"; indivisibility of the transatlantic link; improvement of capabilities; and inclusiveness of all Allies.

2. Author's italics. The White House, Office of the Press Secretary, Press Availability with President Bush and NATO Secretary General Lord Robertson, NATO Headquarters, Brussels, June 13, 2001.

3. See, for instance, Robert Hunter, The European Security and Defense Policy: NATO's Companion—or Competitor? (RAND, 2002); Michael J. Brenner, Europe's New Security Vocation (National Defense University, January 2002).

4. See the essay by Bruno Tertrais on "backfilling" and the "division of labor" debate in this volume.

5. Last year the United States spent 85 per cent more on defense than the other 18 Allies combined, yet in terms of manpower its forces are only half as large as the other Allies combined. See Edgard Buckley, "Attainable targets," NATO Review, Autumn 2002. For a military perspective on U.S. transformation and its possible consequences for transatlantic partnership, see Joseph Ralston, "Keeping NATO's Military Edge Intact in the 21st Century," Speech given at the NATO/German Marshall Fund Conference, October 3, 2002.

6. U.S. Congressional Budget Office, "NATO Burden-sharing After Enlargement," 2001.

7. As Ralph Thiele writes in this volume, 40 shortfalls have been identified in the current European Capability Action Plan, which itself is geared to lower-end operations. "Flexibility through modularity, sustainability, strategic and tactical mobility and firepower are key characteristics of a transformed force capable of meeting tomorrow's threats," Thiele writes, "features seldom found in Europe." For one useful analysis of the capability gap, see David S. Yost, "The NATO Capabilities Gap and the European Union, " Survival, Winter 2000-2001, pp. 87-128.

8. The NATO Response Force emerged from considerable thinking done by both Democratic and Republic defense intellectuals over the past year on the notion of a "spearhead force" as a way to address growing transatlantic divergence. The author participated in one such study group, chaired by former U.S. Ambassador to NATO Robert Hunter and former SACEUR George Joulwan, whose bipartisan report outlines in some detail the nature and goals of such a force. See New Capabilities: Transforming NATO Forces, Atlantic Council of the United States Policy Paper, September 2002.

Conclusion

Esther Brimmer

The volume set out to evaluate the trends behind the EU's European Security and Defense Policy and the implications for transatlantic affairs. Although the book represents the separate views of ten authors the project leads to several conclusions, which in turn lead to recommendations. While the authors support the development of ESDP and suggest ways to improve it, they also realize that significant problems would need to be addressed for ESDP to reach its potential. How these problems are addressed will affect the course of the U.S.-European dialogue on security issues in the coming years.

The chapter authors argue that ESDP is the result of a long and difficult history of efforts to find an expression for European defense cooperation. In this sense, ESDP is the heir to a decades-old process. Thiele, Föhrenbach, and Quinlan explain the role of the ESDP within the EU and its search for an international security role. Finding an EU role in military security would be one of the great milestones in European integration along with the Single Market, the euro, and enlargement. Otte notes that the EU's security role has grown in the 1990s, for example, taking on many of the aspects of the security role envisioned for OSCE. As often advertised by European leaders, the EU could offer a wide range of political, diplomatic, economic and eventually military instruments to exert influence on the parties to a conflict. National governments have some aspects of "one-stop shopping," but the EU offers a chance for a much greater effect given the amount of resources it could bring to bear. Yet the capacities need to fit the mission as Missiroli explains.

As ESDP takes on more tasks it would have to contend with its near neighbor, Russia. It is a hallmark of the times that Russia no longer figures in the EU's evaluations of threats. Forsberg explains the ways in which differences in strategic culture and values impede greater cooperation between the EU and Russia and argues that each is more focused on its relationship with the United States. The way forward may be to look for ways to cooperate on practical long-term projects.

ESDP could have a beneficial impact on the world beyond Europe. If ESDP were successful, it could contribute to international security by enhancing both UN and European capacities to conduct peace-keeping. Esther Brimmer argues that fuller development of the civilian Headline Goals supporting policing and the rule of law in post-conflict zones could be especially helpful, as could initiatives to enhance the EU's capacity for civil protection.

ESDP has already had an impact on transatlantic affairs. Although they have nuanced views, Hamilton, Tertrais, and van Ham broadly agree that the Europeans and Americans can still be partners at times. Despite frictions, European countries along with Canada, Australia and New Zealand, are closer to the U.S. in terms of democratic politics and strategic outlook than any other countries. They share fundamental interests in maintaining open societies based on liberal democracy and market economics. Europeans are realizing that they will have to do more to defend these interests and a world order that supports them. This effort could include not only a political and financial, but—at times—a military commitment. How the EU expresses itself militarily will affect relations with the United States. Although Tertrais argues that there will not be a division of labor between the United States and Europe, the authors raise significant concerns about ESDP and the transatlantic relationship. Van Ham stresses emerging structural strains on the relationship, and Hamilton highlights continuing difficulties with Turkey and potential challenges aligning ESDP and NATO's Response Force initiative.

Some of the transatlantic concerns derive from concerns about ESDP itself. The authors raise issues including:

- *Relevance to future conflicts*

  The challenge of dealing with Iraq, tensions in the greater Middle East, and the campaign against terrorism have raised concerns about ESDP's relevance to future conflicts. At its birth ESDP was influenced by the crises of the recent past including Bosnia and Kosovo. To maintain relevance the EU will need to demonstrate that the combination of civilian and military tools available under ESDP is useful for addressing the types of problems likely to arise in the future.

- *Diminishing political attention to ESDP.*
  Quinlan explains that government leaders seem to have paid less political attention to ESDP in the last two years than during its initial formative period after the France-UK meeting at St. Malo in December 1998 and the EU's 1999 Cologne summit. Enlargement and the European Convention could further distract leaders.

- *Different EU and NATO capabilities requirements.*
  Missiroli notes that there has been a persistent concern over competing standards, initially between the Headline Goals and NATO's DCI. This situation is complicated by the fact that EU members have different national conceptions of what ESDP is. The NATO Response Force presents another category of possibly competing objectives. Having more goals could make meeting any of them harder, or the proliferation of targets could enable governments to pick and choose which ones to meet. Either way the politics of meeting commitments is becoming even more complex.

- *Procurement will be ever more difficult.*
  Missiroli also comments that EU countries will increasingly face awkward decisions about where to procure the major equipment needed for improved capability—whether within Europe, perhaps on a better-coordinated basis than in the past, or from the United States. The debate about the A400M heavy-lift aircraft project is an early illustration of the problem.

- *Yet, there is still a need for integrated conflict management capacities.*
  Brimmer argues that complex emergencies and post-conflict reconstruction demonstrate the continuing need for action by those few countries that can lead the international community. ESDP could help enhance and consolidate European mechanisms for conflict prevention and management.

In their chapters, the authors offer several recommendations for improving ESDP. If it is to be successful it needs to attack its shortcomings. While the details can be found in the chapters, key recommendations include:

- *Resolve the Greece-Turkey impasse.*
  The authors generally agree that the stalemate on use of NATO assets risks stalling ESDP. If the "Berlin-plus" impasse

is not resolved, this could lead to greater NATO-EU decoupling. Without a solution, NATO and hence, the United States, cannot work effectively with the EU on security.

- *Develop shared evaluations of the international situation.*
  The implication of several chapters is that Europeans and Americans need to reexamine their assessments of present and future threats and search for convergent visions of the policy instruments to be used in dealing with these threats.

- *Strengthen NATO Secretary General and EU High Representative for CFSP.*
  In light of the dual enlargement of both the EU and NATO, both institutions could benefit from mechanisms for consensus building by strengthening the executive functions of the respective international structures and their heads. Marc Otte suggests that the NATO Secretary General and the EU High Representative be given increased means of action. However, this is a sensitive point touching on political control by member states and on leadership within each institution.

- *Replace the rotating presidency.*
  Authors discuss the idea of replacing the rotating EU presidency system with a more efficient system.

- *Improve the provision of capabilities including:*
  - Missiroli outlines additional incentives for a) getting higher value for money (spending *better*), and b) freeing more resources for "defense" (spending more) by some pooling of defense expenditure.

  - In the longer term, this can be done through some role specialisation for both capabilities/forces and assets/materiel. This could imply the allocation of specific functional roles to certain member States.

  - In the medium term, this could be achieved through a common (but not necessarily a single) procurement policy and a less protected market for defense industry.

- In the short term, this could be done through the creation of some EU-funded supranational force elements. An interesting model in this same field is the one adopted by NATO for its AWACS aircraft. Missiroli suggests a "European Defense Fund" to fill the existing gap between the general willingness to cooperate and the lack of available and reliable on-call resources. He also recommends creating some common principles that could be agreed to measure national contributions to ESDP: such as money, assets, manpower, and know-how. Additional concerns would focus on the potential for exclusion of non-EU members from such arrangements,

- *Interpret the Petersberg tasks.*
  Several authors explained that the scope of the "Petersberg tasks" is not interpreted in the same way inside the EU. There certainly is a broad consensus over their "low-end," for which most of the necessary resources are already available. "High-end" missions, however, are much more controversial and their understanding seems different even among the six main military players in the EU.

- *Make ESDP and the NATO Response Force complementary, not competitive*
  ESDP and the NATO Response Force could be developed to enhance the range of capabilities available to prevent and manage conflicts, if leaders so choose. However, this effort would require that the Berlin-plus impasse be resolved and an effective NATO-EU working relationship be created. States that are members of both the EU and NATO would need to help build this relationship.

On the one hand, EU leaders need to decide whether ESDP is intended to project military power beyond Europe. If so, it would need additional specialized military capabilities. If not, and it only would be deployed in actions in or near Europe, then more modest equipment enhancements are needed. Europeans need to consider whether ESDP should be modified in light of the reemergence of national capitals after September 11 and the proposed NATO Response Force. On the other hand, Americans need to think hard about how they would like to work with Europe in military operations. It remains to be seen how NRF and ESDP could be mutually reinforcing.

Europeans and Americans have to rethink their understandings of when and how to use force. They also need to examine their contrasting approaches to crisis management. While national governments will continue to take the lead on key strategic issues, the EU could stake its claim to addressing complex emergencies that demand a blend of military action, civil protection, development aid, international civilian policing, and the restoration of the rule of law. From Macedonia to Afghanistan, there are many situations that could benefit from increased international capacity to prevent and manage complex crises. As American policymakers discover how much these skills are needed today, they may develop a greater appreciation for the EU's evolving security role.

Although their views vary, overall the authors agree that an improvement in Europe's capacity to act militarily, as well as to manage civilian crises, would provide the foundations for a viable long-term transatlantic partnership. Such a partnership is a goal valued by many Europeans and Americans alike, and potentially beneficial for global security as a whole.

Afterword

Dr. Klaus Scharioth

State Secretary, German Foreign Office

Themes of his keynote speech on the occasion of the final meeting of
the strategy group on European Security and Defense Policy (ESDP):
Implications for Transatlantic Relations

Berlin, October 1, 2002

Making ESDP strong will strengthen NATO and the Transatlantic Partnership

Summary

Shaping globalization in order to promote stability and progress
around the world requires a European Union capable of playing its
full role on the international stage; to this end, the Union is supple-
menting its broad array of foreign policy instruments with capabilities
for international conflict prevention and crisis management through
its European Security and Defense Policy (ESDP). Yet ESDP is crucial not only for strengthening Europe's capacity to act but also for
strengthening transatlantic partnership. These objectives are, in fact,
two sides of the same coin. Only a united and strong Europe will be a
strong and attractive partner for the United States. Just as much as a
strong America is good for Europe, a strong Europe is good for
America. Only a Europe with effective military capabilities will be
taken seriously by the United States as well as other partners and will
have a greater say in transatlantic relations. This does not require
imitating U.S. military might; Europe is not and does not aspire to
become a global military power. Rather, the aim is to secure transatlantic interoperability; hence, reducing the capability gap is not an end
in itself but a means to achieving interoperability.

ESDP enjoys solid public support: polls show that Europeans want
a Europe capable of acting in the field of security policy. NATO

remains essential for our common security and a bedrock of transatlantic partnership in the future. The Kosovo conflict has demonstrated that a U.S.-European discrepancy in capabilities can pose a serious threat to NATO's cohesion. Therefore, to keep NATO vital, Europeans must become stronger. ESDP aims at realizing President Kennedy's vision of a two-pillar Alliance, i.e. at strengthening NATO. The objective is to establish a genuine strategic partnership between the EU and NATO.

To expound the implications of ESDP for transatlantic relations, three main issues will be discussed in greater detail:

- The importance of the ESDP project,

- What has been achieved up to date,

- The challenges Europe will have to meet to render ESDP successful and thus strengthen NATO and the transatlantic partnership.

Importance of ESDP project

Following the introduction of the euro, ESDP is the next great European project. It has four main features:

- *Strengthening Europe's capacity to act*
  Shaping globalization to promote stability and progress around the world is the crucial task and challenge of the 21st century. The essence of shaping globalization is setting and maintaining agreed rules in international relations. The attacks on September 11, 2001, are the starkest reminder yet that international terrorism is one of the gravest threats to our common security. Coping with this threat requires a broad international anti-terrorist coalition, as noted clearly in the recently published U.S. National Security Strategy: "While or focus is protecting America, we know that to defeat terrorism in today's globalized world we need support from our allies and friends." The same is true for the crucial task of shaping globalization. This challenge as well as the threat posed by international terrorism require a European Union capable of acting as one: no single EU member state is powerful enough to influence significantly the course and contents of globaliza-

tion. This, again, reveals one of the driving forces of European integration: by pooling sovereignty member states are able to regain sovereignty they would not have as individual nations.

The Union has long had at its disposal a wide range of political, economic and financial instruments enabling it to pursue the interests of its member states on the international stage. What it lacks are military and civilian means for international crisis management that would give the Common Foreign and Security Policy (CFSP) additional substance and profile. By launching the ESDP project at the European Council in Cologne in June 1999, EU member states have set out to develop such capabilities in order to further strengthen the Union's capacity to act.

- *Conflict prevention and crisis management*
  Promoting the non-violent settlement of conflicts has always been a core Union priority. ESDP capabilities will serve both these objectives: to prevent the outbreak of violence (conflict prevention) and, if this cannot be achieved, to contain and end a violent conflict as quickly as possible (crisis management).

- *Crisis management using military and civilian means*
  A "trademark" and peculiar strength of the ESDP is the parallel and balanced development of military and civilian capabilities, the latter focusing on police, rule of law, civilian administration and civil protection capacities. The Balkan conflicts of the past decade have demonstrated that only this combination of military and civilian capabilities permits effective crisis management.

- *Strengthening NATO and the transatlantic partnership*
  Transatlantic conflicts should not make us forget but rather remind us of a fundamental feature of international politics: Europe and America are indispensable partners in shaping globalization because of common values and interests together with our combined political and economic weight. Consequently, a Europe becoming stronger through developing an effective ESDP will help to strengthen the transatlantic partnership and to keep NATO vital.

Taking stock: What has been achieved up to date?

Beauty, it has been said, lies in the eyes of the beholder. In international politics, it is perceptions that matter when it comes to assessing the success or failure of political strategies and projects. Regarding ESDP, frequently the exclusive focus is on the empty part of the half-full glass. That is rather unfair.

To be sure ESDP still has a long way to go. It is still in its "infancy," and crucial tests still have to be passed. Yet a fair assessment also has to take account of that part of the glass which is no longer empty.

Giving due credit to the project has to start with considering that an effective ESDP requires both a capacity to act and a readiness to act. Where do we stand on these two issues?

Capabilities

Americans, it is being said, are interested in three things when it comes to ESDP: capabilities, capabilities, capabilities. Understandably enough: ESDP is a project designed to redress shortfalls and to fill gaps. The aim is to enable the Union to carry out crisis management operations along the full spectrum of the so-called "Petersberg tasks" set out in the Treaty on European Union: "humanitarian and rescue tasks, peace-keeping tasks and tasks of combat forces in crisis management, including peacemaking." The method chosen to achieve this end is the establishment of targets member states are committed to reach jointly.

- *Military Capabilities*

  European Headline goal: In Helsinki in December 1999, EU member states agreed that they must be able, by 2003, to deploy within 60 days and sustain for at least 1 year military forces of up to 50,000-60,000 persons, with additional air and naval elements as required;

  Collective capability goals were established simultaneously in the fields of command and control, intelligence and strategic transport; the purpose of these goals is to mobilize member states' collective efforts to remedy shortcomings in fields of crucial importance for Petersberg-type missions;

Capabilities Commitment Conference in November 2000: member states pledged over 100,000 persons as well as some 400 combat aircraft and 100 ships for Petersberg-type operations;

Capabilities Improvement Conference in November 2001 adopted a European Capabilities Action Plan to identify specific ways and means of remedying critical shortcomings. The conference confirmed that due to progress made so far, the EU should be able to carry out the whole range of Petersberg tasks by 2003.

* *Civilian Capabilities*

   Targets have also been set for the creation of civilian capabilities. This was done against the backdrop of the Balkan conflicts, which showed that it is more difficult to recruit police officers, judges and civil administrators than soldiers. That is why developing civilian capabilities is so crucial.

At the Feira European Council in June 2000, EU member states agreed that they must be able, by 2003, to make available up to 5,000 police officers (1,000 of which within 30 days) for EU contributions to missions led by international organizations (UN, OSCE) or for autonomous EU missions. A Commitment Conference held in November 2001 made clear these targets were likely to be met (with 910 officers, Germany is providing the second largest contingent).

Further civilian capability targets were adopted in June 2001:

   * availability of up to 200 experts in the rule of law field (judges, prosecutors, correctional officers); at a commitment conference in May 2002, member states pledged 282 experts (including 72 judges), with Germany providing the largest contingent of 60 experts.

   * establishment of a pool of experts able to undertake civilian administration tasks;

   * availability of civil protection intervention teams of up to 2,000 persons that can be deployed at very short notice.

We are confident to reach all of these targets by 2003.

Readiness to Act

- *Operationality*

  The Laeken European Council held in December 2001 adopted a "Declaration on the Operational Capability of ESDP." The EU is now operational, but with two crucial caveats. Due to continuing critical shortfalls in military capabilities, at this stage the Union is able to conduct only "some" crisis-management operations, i.e., less than the most demanding Petersberg-type operations. Consequently, the level of operationality will increase along with increasing capabilities.

- *Operations*

  The next important step to take in order to advance the ESDP project is moving from building-up capabilities to making use of capabilities—when it is necessary and when it is in conformity with the interests and values of EU member states.

  Police Mission: The first civilian operation has been agreed upon: from 2003, the EU will conduct a police mission in Bosnia and Herzegovina as a follow-on to the current UN mission, the International Police Task Force (IPTF).

  Military Mission: In the military field, the Union has expressed its willingness to take over from NATO in the Former Yugoslav Republic of Macedonia (FYROM). The principal reasons being that an EU military engagement would complement the substantial non-military assistance the EU has provided to that country, the stabilizing effect of the international community's military presence, the scale of NATO's current mission ("Task Force Fox") and American expectations that Europeans take on a larger share of the common burden, particularly in the Balkans. A prerequisite for an EU takeover is the prior conclusion of EU-NATO permanent arrangements ("Berlin Plus") on EU access to NATO assets and capabilities. Once these agreements will have been achieved, the EU could launch its first military operation—provided, of course, that the FYROM government would issue such a request.

Challenges

While ESDP is better than its reputation in certain quarters, much remains to be done to render it successful. Five areas are crucial in this regard:

- *Capabilities*
  To a decisive degree, the fate of the ESDP project hinges on reaching our targets and putting our resources where our mouths are. In the same vein, improving our capabilities is also crucial for maintaining and restoring transatlantic interoperability, a consideration that again underscores the importance of the ESDP project for a more balanced and vital NATO Alliance.

  Therefore, what is needed is 'political sustainability', i.e. a long-term common European effort to address shortcomings that have accumulated over many years. Money, however, will remain a scarce resource; therefore, the success of ESDP will depend crucially on spending money more wisely. Today, the 15 EU member states spend almost 60 per cent of what the United States spends on defense but their output in terms of military capabilities is much less than that. Consequently, we need to become much more efficient through increased pooling of resources and role specialization.

  Pooling resources means pooling sovereignty and the loss of national autonomy; however, the value added through pooling and de-nationalization consists of a collective capacity to act that no individual member state would have and that would be difficult to create through "ad-hocery." Germany is prepared to go further down this route of shared sovereignty.

- *Operations*
  Creating capabilities is one side, using them the other side of the coin of making ESDP effective. It is rather to be expected that a world shrinking through globalization will remain a turbulent place containing multiple threats to our security and well-being. Political extremism, fundamentalist ideologies, international terrorism, the spread of weapons technology and of weapons of mass destruction, the vulnerability of modern societies and economies to rather "primitive" means of

destruction as shown on September 11—these elements add up to a perilous mixture of risks and challenges.

Preventing and confronting threats to our security is an integral part of shaping and managing globalization. Whenever and wherever possible we should deal with these challenges in a preventive, non-violent mode. However, as the Balkan wars that led to the launching of the ESDP have painfully taught us: there can be situations where military means might be needed as part of a political strategy to preserve or restore peace.

Against this background of, on the one hand, a Europe that has values to promote and interests to defend in shaping globalization and, on the other hand, a world that will not offer Europe the luxury of retreating to an "island of the blessed," I venture the prediction that Europe will muster the political will to carry out operations when the situation calls for it and when it is in our interest.

- *Third States*

  ESDP is an open project. We welcome the participation of non-EU states in EU-led operations, notably non-EU NATO states and other EU candidate countries (thus, about 16 non-EU states will participate in the EU Police Mission in Bosnia and Herzegovina as of January 1, 2003). On the other hand, it is important to ensure that the EU's credibility and ability to act are not diminished by the involvement of third parties in ESDP operations.

- *Enlargement*

  Enlargement raises the question of the capacity to act of a Union with 25 or even more members. The prospect of enlargement is one more reason why Germany is in favor of making qualified majority voting the rule in matters of Common Foreign and Security Policy. However, this will not be possible when it comes to such extremely sensitive issues as defense and military operations. Therefore, in these cases the flexibility needed should be provided for by introducing the possibility of enhanced cooperation in the field of ESDP. If not all member states want to be part of a particular action or project those who want to go ahead should be able to do so without the others preventing them from doing so.

• *EU-NATO cooperation*
To repeat: Europe and America are indispensable partners in shaping globalization.

The challenge is to establish a real strategic partnership in the field of security policy. Partnership cuts both ways: Europeans must get their act together and improve their capabilities, and Americans must respect that a corollary of burden-sharing is power-sharing. Ultimately, this could lead to realizing the Kennedy vision of a two-pillar NATO.

There are, however, two more immediate tasks to be solved in order to establish a solid basis for EU-NATO cooperation.

The first one is building an EU-NATO bridge through "Berlin Plus" permanent arrangements, i.e. assured EU access to NATO's planning capabilities, presumption of availability of pre-identified NATO assets and capabilities for EU-led operations, and DSACEUR as EU operations commander. Such arrangements are imperative for several reasons: they buttress a strategic EU-NATO partnership with NATO continuing to be responsible for our collective defense and they provide an important additional transatlantic link; they obviate unnecessary and wasteful duplication of scarce resources.

The second immediate task is to take care that developments of military capabilities within NATO and the EU remain mutually reinforcing. This, too, cuts both ways: the evolution of ESDP must be compatible with commitments taken on within NATO, and NATO developments must, to the extent that EU and NATO missions overlap, continue to support EU objectives. The reasons are obvious: We only have a single set of forces and the EU and NATO must be able to cooperate smoothly. A case in point is the American proposal to set up a NATO Response Force. Developing such a capability has great potential for strengthening the Alliance and its capacity to deal with new threats. To fully realize this potential, reinforcing the EU-NATO strategic partnership is an important objective, too.

Conclusion

ESDP is of crucial importance to the future of NATO and the transatlantic relationship. Today, one of the key challenges facing the Alliance is the maintenance and restoration of U.S.-European interoperability. Meeting this challenge requires improving European military capabilities and reconfiguring our military forces so that they are able to deal with future threats and risks. The ESDP project offers a great chance to accelerate this process and create a Europe capable of playing its full and appropriate role on the international stage. By developing capabilities that will supplement the already broad range of instruments at the disposal of the European Union, Europe will become a stronger partner in a transatlantic relationship that remains indispensable for our common security and for shaping globalization to our mutual benefit.

Basic Concepts of European Defense Policy

Bruno Tertrais

Strictly speaking, "ESDP" is a concept born and developed in the European Union (EU), referring to the defense and security dimension of the EU's common foreign policy. But issues of European defense policy and European military operations involve also other bodies, in particular the North Atlantic Treaty Organization (NATO), as well as European multinational forces.

The European Union

The Treaty on the European Union, also known as the **Maastricht** treaty (1992), transformed the European Communities into a **European Union** (EU) made of three components known as "pillars": a single European Community (first pillar); the Common Foreign and Security Policy (second pillar); and cooperation on Justice and Home Affairs (third pillar). The Treaty on the European Union was subsequently modified by the **Amsterdam** (1997) and **Nice** (2001) treaties.

Unlike European Community policies, the CFSP is an intergovernmental process, conducted by the EU states through the **European Council** (Heads of State or Government) and the **Council of the European Union** meeting as "General Affairs Council" (Foreign Ministers). Thus the **High Representative for CFSP**, a position created by the Amsterdam treaty and currently held by Mr. Javier Solana, reports to the Council, and not to the Commission.[1] CFSP initiatives come mostly from the Presidency of the Union, from the Member States, and from the High Representative. As its name indicates, it is a "common" policy and not a "single" one: it does not replace national foreign and security policies.

The Maastricht treaty also envisaged *"the eventual framing of a common defense policy which might in time lead to a common defense."* The Amsterdam treaty went one step further by mentioning the *"progressive"* framing of such a policy.[2] Political impetus for the development of a European defense policy was given by the **Saint-Malo** British-French summit of December 1998 and by the Kosovo crisis. The **Cologne** Council meeting (June 1999) thus decided that *"the Union must have the capacity for autonomous action, backed up by credible military forces, and a readiness to do so, in order to respond to international crises without prejudice to actions by NATO."*

Concept

At the **Helsinki** Council meeting (December 1999), the EU members committed themselves to develop a *"the Union's military and non-military crisis management capability as part of a strengthened common European policy on security and defense,"* and underlined their determination to develop *"an autonomous capacity to take decisions and, where NATO as a whole is not engaged, to launch and conduct EU-led military operations in response to international crises."*

Missions

The EU military missions, known as the **Petersberg tasks**, were defined in the Amsterdam treaty: *"humanitarian and rescue tasks, peacekeeping tasks and tasks of combat forces in crisis management, including peacemaking."*[3] Crisis management also includes the civilian dimension; in particular, as defined at the **Feira** Council meeting of June 2000, the areas of police, rule of law, civilian administration, and civil protection.

Structures

To plan for, organize and supervise military operations, the EU decided in Nice to set up a **Political and Security Committee** (PSC) as well as **European Military Committee** (EUMC) supported by a 135 strong **European Military Staff** (EUMS), for early warning, situation assessment and strategic planning. For the civilian dimension a **Committee for Civilian Aspects of Crisis Management** (CivCom) has been set up, along with a **Police Unit** in the Secretariat.

Assets

- The **Headline Goal** adopted in Helsinki stated that member States should be able, by 2003, to deploy within 60 days, and sustain for at least a year, military forces of up to 50,000-60,000 personnel, with additional air and naval elements as necessary. Such forces will be drawn from a pool of forces made available by member States representing a total of 100,000 personnel, about 400 combat aircraft, and 100 warships, as stated at the **Nice** Council meeting (2000). A **Helsinki Headline Goal Catalogue** (HHC) was drawn up to list capabilities needed; national contributions forming the EU's reservoir of forces were pledged at the **Capabilities Commitment Conference** (November 2000), and summarized in a **Helsinki Force Catalogue** (HFC). Following the **Capabilities Improvement Conference** (November 2001), a **European Capabilities Action Plan** was adopted.

- The European Union does not have its own operational command structures. For operational planning and military conduct of an operation, the Union would rely either on NATO assets and C3, or on national assets using the concept of **lead nation.**

- At the **Feira** meeting, member States agreed to provide, by 2003, up to 5,000 police personnel, including 1,000 to be deployed within 30 days, for conflict prevention and crisis management operations. A **Police Capabilities, Commitment Conference** was held in November 2001.

- Also, at the **Göteborg** European Council meeting of June 2001, the following set of targets was identified: up to 200 experts of the rule of law (such as judges); a pool of experts for civilian administration; and the availability of civil protection intervention teams of up to 2,000 on short notice. A **Rule of Law Capabilities Commitment Conference** was held in May 2002.

- The Union also has an **EU Satellite Center** and an **EU Situation Center.**

In December 2001, at the **Laeken** Council meeting, the achievement of setting up structures and procedures for European operations allowed the EU to declare itself *"operational"* for crisis management operations.

NATO

The idea of a **European Security and Defense Identity** (ESDI) within the Atlantic Alliance was first mentioned in the 1990 "Declaration on A Transformed Alliance" adopted at the London NATO Summit: *"The move within the European Community towards political union, including the development of a European identity in the domain of security, will also contribute to Atlantic solidarity and to the establishment of a just and lasting order of peace throughout the whole of Europe."*

In 1993, the concept of **Combined Joint Task Forces** (CJTF) was devised by the United States as a way to generate *ad hoc* forces, making NATO a more flexible military instrument, including for European use of NATO assets. Alliance agreement on the concept was formalized at the January 1994 Brussels Summit, which recognized the importance of the ESDI.

In 1996, the **Berlin** agreement between NATO and the WEU defined the relationship between the two organizations. The Alliance subscribed to the possibility of generating CJTF led by Europeans. The **Deputy-SACEUR** (who has always been a European) was to have a key role for European military operations using NATO assets, including as a probable theatre or operation commander.

In 1999, Alliance members agreed to develop arrangements allowing for: *"assured EU access to NATO planning capabilities"*; *"the presumption of availability to the EU of pre-identified NATO capabilities and common assets"* such as HQs, C3I, and AWACS; enhancing the role of the D-SACEUR, as a potential operational commander of an EU-led operation and as ESDI strategic coordinator within NATO; and adapting NATO's defense planning system to incorporate the availability of forces for EU-led operations. These arrangements are known as **Berlin plus**.

Other institutions

The Western European Union

The 1948 **Brussels treaty** signed originally by five European countries included an **Article 5** that stipulated that an attack against one Party was to be considered an attack against all Parties and met with a common military response. However, when the Washington Treaty was signed in 1949, the Parties to the Brussels Treaty agreed to transfer its collective defense function to NATO. In 1954, the Brussels treaty was modified to create a **Western European Union** (WEU) which was seen as the EU's "secular arm" for defense policy from 1992 until 1999, as well as a "bridge" between NATO and the EU.

In June 1999, at the **Cologne** meeting, member States decided to transfer to the EU the WEU structures and procedures for military operations. The WEU remains as a caretaker organization for the Brussels Treaty, and as a coordinating body for armaments cooperation (see below). It involves those ten countries which are both members of the EU and NATO.[4] Thus these ten EU countries are bound both by the Washington treaty's Article 5 and by the Brussels treaty's own Article 5 (which is slightly more demanding since it explicitly mentions military assistance).

Cooperation on military equipments

The **Western European Armaments Group** (WEAG), created in 1992, is an armaments cooperation forum now involving 19 EU and non-EU countries. It directs the work of the **Western European Armaments Organization** (WEAO), a subsidiary body of the WEU established in 1996, mostly devoted to research and policy planning.

Two smaller, but also more focused circles of cooperation exist:

- The group of nations which signed in 1998 the so-called **Letter of Intent** (LoI): France, Germany, Italy, Spain, Sweden and the UK. The goal is to facilitate cooperation, industrial regroupings, and the management of common programs, by simplifying and harmonizing the legal rules applicable to defense industries.

- The *Organisme Conjoint de Coopération en matière d'Armement* (OCCAR), an organization created in 1998, which includes France, Germany, Italy and the UK. Its role is to manage common equipments programs.

Also noteworthy is the **FINABEL** group created in 1953, which seeks to enhance the interoperability of European land forces. It involves the military staffs of France, Italy, the Netherlands, Germany, Belgium, the United Kingdom, Spain, Greece, and Portugal.

Multinational Forces

Since the end of the Cold War, the Europeans have set up new multinational military formations which are not formally assigned to the EU or NATO but could be made available, if need be, to any of the two, or used independently. The most significant of these forces are: the **Eurocorps** (1991), which today comprises division-size Belgian, French and German elements, Spanish and Luxemburg forces, and the **French-German Brigade**; the **Eurofor** (1995), a non-permanent four-brigade rapid reaction force made up of French, Italian, Portuguese and Spanish forces; the **Euromarfor** (1995), a non-permanent maritime force made up of French, Italian, Portuguese and Spanish units, with no dedicated HQ; the **European Air Group** (1998), a light planning and coordinating structure involving France, Germany, Italy and the UK, and which includes, since 2001, a **European Air Transport Coordination Cell.**

Notes:

1. He is also the Secretary-General of the Council.

2. The Treaty on the European Union, as amended by the Nice treaty, now reads as follows: *"Article 17. 1. The common foreign and security policy shall include all questions relating to the security of the Union, including the progressive framing of a common defense policy, which might lead to a common defense, should the European Council so decide."*

3. The name Petersberg refers to the meeting place near Bonn, Germany, where, in June 1992, the WEU members agreed on a text defining future European military missions. It is this text which was included in the Amsterdam Treaty.

4. All EU members except five countries: Austria, Ireland, Sweden (neutrals), Finland (non-aligned), and Denmark (which has chosen to "opt out" of the EU's defense policy).

About the Authors

Dr. Esther Brimmer is Deputy Director and Director of Research at the Center for Transatlantic Relations at the Paul H. Nitze School of Advanced International Studies at the Johns Hopkins University. In fall 2001, she was a DAAD Research Fellow at the American Institute for Contemporary German Studies also at the Johns Hopkins University in Washington, D.C. From 1999-2001, she was a Member of the Office of Policy Planning at the U.S. Department of State. Previously she was a Senior Associate at the Carnegie Commission on Preventing Deadly Conflict. From 1993-1995 she served as a Special Assistant to the Under Secretary of State for Political Affairs. She wrote weekly analyses of foreign affairs and defense issues for members of Congress and their staffs as a Legislative Analyst at the Democratic Study Group in the U.S. House of Representatives from 1991-1993. She received her D.Phil. (Ph.D.) and master's degrees in international relations from the University of Oxford.

Dr. Gerd Föhrenbach is the Deputy Head of the Law/Politics Division at the Bundeswehr Center for Analyses and Studies. He studied political science, history and English at the University of Freiburg (Germany) and at the University of Massachusetts in Amherst (USA). From 1997-99 he was a Junior Fellow at the Center for European Integration Studies, Bonn. During 1998/99 he was the Chancellor Kohl Research Associate at the Center for German and European Studies, Georgetown University, Washington, DC. Dr. Föhrenbach received his Ph.D. in political science at the University of Freiburg. His various publications include works on U.S. foreign policy, transatlantic relations, and security in the Baltic Sea region.

Dr. Tuomas Forsberg is a Professor in the Western European Security Studies College of International and Security Studies at the George C. Marshall European Center for Security Studies in Garmisch-Partenkirchen, Germany. Previously he was director of research at the Finnish Institute of International Affairs. He is the author of numerous articles on strategic issues.

Dr. Daniel S. Hamilton is Richard von Weizsaecker Professor and Director of the Center for Transatlantic Relations at the Paul H.

Nitze School of Advanced International Studies (SAIS) at the Johns Hopkins University. He is also Executive Director of the American Consortium on EU Studies (ACES), a five-university consortium that is the EU Center in Washington, DC. He has served as Deputy Assistant Secretary of State for European Affairs, responsible for U.S. policy toward European security, including ESDP and NATO issues. He also served as U.S. Special Coordinator for Northern Europe; U.S. Special Coordinator for Southeast European Stabilization, Associate Director of the Policy Planning Staff for two secretaries of state, Policy Adviser to Assistant Secretary of State for European Affairs Richard C. Holbrooke, and Senior Policy Adviser to Ambassador Holbrooke and the U.S. Embassy in Germany. He has been a Senior Fellow at the Carnegie Endowment for International Peace and Deputy Director of the Aspen Institute Berlin. He received his Ph.D and M.A. from Johns Hopkins SAIS, and B.S. from Georgetown University.

Dr. Antonio Missiroli is a Research Fellow at the European Union's Institute for Security Studies in Paris. He received a doctorate in contemporary history from the Scuola Normale Superiore, Pisa and a Master of International Public Policy from the Johns Hopkins University. From 1993 to 1996, he was a lecturer in West European Politics at Dickinson College, in the United States and in Bologna, as well as Head of European Studies, CeSPI, Rome. From 1996 to 1997, he was a British Council Visiting Fellow at St. Antony's College, Oxford. His publications include papers on CFSP, Scandinavia, political opposition, Central Europe and Italian foreign policy and four books entitled *Die Deutsche Hochschule für Politik*, *La questione tedesca*, *Les deux Allemagnes*, and *Dove nascono le elites in Europa*.

Ambassador Marc Otte is Head of the ESDP Task Force in the EU Policy Planning and Early Warning Unit for the General Secretariat of the Council of the European Union, Brussels. He is an advisor on defense and security policy to the High Representative for Common Foreign and Security Policy. In his diplomatic career, Amb. Otte has served as Director for Security Policy and Disarmament, General Directorate for Political Affairs, Belgian Ministry of Foreign Affairs; Ambassador of Belgium to Israel; and Consul General of Belgium in Los Angeles, as well as in other posts in the Belgian embassies in Washington, D.C. and in Kinshasa, Zaire. He received his MA in

Political and Social Sciences from the University of Louvain in 1969 and a post graduate degree from the Institute for Developing Countries, University of Louvain, in 1970. His publications include "Perspectives pour la Défense Européenne après le Sommet de Cologne"; Centre for Defense Studies, Royal Institute for Defense, Brussels (December 1999).

Sir Michael Quinlan was a United Kingdom civil servant from 1954 to 1992, mostly in the defense field. He was secretary of the Eurogroup from 1970 to 1973, and his final governmental appointment was as Permanent Under-Secretary of State for Defense. He was Director of the Ditchley Foundation from 1992 to 1999. He has written "European Defense Cooperation," published by the Woodrow Wilson Center. He is a Visiting Professor in the Department of War Studies, King's College London.

Dr. Bruno Tertrais is a Senior Research Fellow at the Fondation pour la Recherche Stratégique in Paris. He graduated from the Institut d'études politiques de Paris in 1984. He also holds a Master's degree in Public Law (1985), and a Doctorate in Political Science (1994). Between 1990 and 1993, he was Director of the Civilian Affairs Committee, NATO Assembly, Brussels. In 1993, he joined the Délégation aux Affaires stratégiques (Policy Division) of the French Ministry of Defense. In 1995-1996, he was a Visiting Fellow at RAND, Santa Monica. From 1996 until 2001, he was Special Assistant to the Director of Strategic Affairs at the French Ministry of Defense. His publications include *Nuclear Policies in Europe* (Oxford University Press, 1999); *US Missile Defense: Strategically Sound, Politically Questionable* (Center for European Reform, 2001); *L'Asie nucléaire* (Institut français de relations internationales, 2001) He is also a Lecturer in World Politics at the Institut d'études politiques de Paris.

Colonel Ralph D. Thiele is the Commander of the Bundeswehr Center for Analyses and Studies. He has been directly involved in numerous national and NATO strategic issues while serving as executive officer to the Bundeswehr Vice Chief of Defense Staff, Military Assistant to the Supreme Allied Commander Europe, and in the Planning and Policy Staff of the German Minister of Defense and as Chief of Staff NATO Defense College. Col. Thiele has published several books and articles for military and academic publications and lectured widely in Europe and in the U.S. on security affairs and German security policy. He is a member of the "Deutsche Atlantische Gesellschaft" (German Atlantic Association) and the chairman of the "Politisch-Militärische Gesellschaft" (Political-Military Society).

Dr. Peter van Ham is a Senior Research Fellow at the Netherlands Institute of International Relations "Clingendael" in The Hague and a professor at the College of Europe in Bruges. From 1996-2001 he was Professor of West European Politics at the George C. Marshall European Center for Security Studies in Garmisch-Partenkirchen, Germany. From 1993-1996 he was a Senior Research Fellow at the WEU Institute for Security Studies in Paris. His recent books include *Mapping European Security After Kosovo* (Manchester University Press, 2002); *European Integration and the Postmodern Condition* (Routledge, 2001) and A *Critical Approach to European Security* (Pinter, 1999). He also published in *The National Interest, Foreign Affairs, Security Dialogue, European Security* and *Millennium*.

About the Center

The Center for Transatlantic Relations is based at The Johns Hopkins University Paul H. Nitze School of Advanced International Studies in Washington, D.C. The Center engages international scholars, government officials, journalists, business executives, and other opinion leaders from both sides of the Atlantic on issues facing Europe and North America. Center activities include research projects, policy study groups, publications, seminars and lectures, media programs, and web-based activities. The Center also serves as the coordinator for the five-university American Consortium on European Union Studies (ACES), which has been designated by the European Union as one of a select group of Centers for European Union Studies in the United States. More information is available at http://transatlantic.sais-jhu.edu.